L AND NOTHING

UNTIMELY MEDITATIONS

ALL AND NOTHING

A DIGITAL APOCALYPSE

MARTIN BURCKHARDT
DIRK HÖFER

THE MIT PRESS
CAMBRIDGE, MASSACHUSETTS
LONDON, ENGLAND

TRANSLATED BY ERIK BUTLER

Originally published as *Alles und Nichts: Ein Pandämonium digitaler Weltvernichtung* in the series *Fröhliche Wissenschaft* by Matthes & Seitz Berlin: © Matthes & Seitz Berlin Verlagsgesellschaft mbH, Berlin 2015. All rights reserved.

The translation of this work was supported by a grant from the Goethe-Institut.

This book was set in PF DIN Text Pro by Toppan Best-set Premedia Limited. Printed and bound in the United States of America.

Library of Congress Cataloging-in-Publication Data

Names: Burckhardt, Martin. | Höfer, Dirk, 1956- | Butler, Erik, 1971- translator.
Title: All and nothing : a pandemonium of digital world destruction / Martin Burckhardt and Dirk Höfer ; translated by Erik Butler.
Other titles: Alles und Nichts. English
Description: Cambridge, MA : The MIT Press, [2017] | Series: Untimely meditations | Includes bibliographical references.
Identifiers: LCCN 2017002616 | ISBN 9780262534253 (pbk. : alk. paper)
Subjects: LCSH: Digital media. | Information society. | Philosophy and civilization. | Nothing (Philosophy)
Classification: LCC B54 .B8713 2017 | DDC 100--dc23 LC record available at https://lccn.loc.gov/2017002616

10   9   8   7   6   5   4   3   2   1

CONTENTS

ALL AND NOTHING

1 REVELATION

Boole and the Formula

In the beginning was the Zero, and the Zero was with God, and God was the One. The Zero and the One were with God in the beginning. Through them all things were made; without them nothing was made that has been made. In them was life, and life was the light of men. The light shines in the darkness, but the darkness has not understood it.

In 1854, the British mathematician George Boole published *Investigations of the Laws of Thought*. The author had experienced an ecstatic vision in his youth that set the course for his intellectual life. The book presented the idea of a universe whose elements could be understood in terms of the logic of presence or absence: 0 or 1. In Boolean algebra, the world of numbers—and along with it, the world as a whole—breaks down into binary code.[1] Numbers as we

1. The first mention of a binary number system was made by Gottfried Wilhelm Leibniz, who offered a *theologoumenon*: "Whereas one of the principle articles of the Christian faith ... is the creation of all things from nothing through God's omnipotence, one may duly affirm that nothing in the world shows as much—indeed, proves as much, as it were—than the origin of numbers as presented here: through One and Zero (or Nothing), strictly and solely, do all numbers arise. It would be difficult to find a better example of this mystery in nature or philosophy. ... The matter proves all the more opportune for us here inasmuch as the empty depths and barren darkness belong to Zero and Nothing, and the Spirit of God, with its Light, to the all-powerful One. I reflected at length on the words for the allegory and finally deemed the following verse meet: 'To draw everything from nothing, One is enough (*Omnibus ex nihilo ducendis sufficit unum*).'" Letter to Duke Rudolf von Braunschweig-Wolfenbüttel, January 2, 1697.

know them are forms through which this coding manifests itself. In other words, they do not *represent* anything. The Boolean digits 1 and 0 do not designate a quantity; instead, they mark presence and absence. Thus, 1 stands for the universe, and 0 stands for nothingness. Nevertheless, the terms are not governed by a mutually exclusive relationship. Their relationship is complementary: they follow the same logic. Just as 1 times 1 always yields 1, and 0 times 0 always produces 0, x times x always equals x in the Boolean world. For the same reason, All and Nothing meet up in the formula $x = x^n$. Because x can stand for anything and everything—indeed, for the universe in its entirety—it is no exaggeration to speak of a *digital world formula* in this context.

The world may be conceived as a vast magnet oscillating between a positive pole and a negative pole, that is, in terms of dyadic logic. This perspective is rife with significance, for whatever can be electrified can also be digitized. Accordingly, x may stand for an alphanumeric sign, a sound file, or an image; it may just as readily indicate the level of hemoglobin in one's blood as measured by a sensor, or the coordinates of a migrating whale. Indeed, it may stand for all we have yet to digitize in the future: our speech acts, emotions, and dreams. At any rate, when it is digitized, a given x no longer stands as a singularity, an isolated entity; the formula allows us to duplicate it at will. In fact, x duplicates itself on its own: it turns into a *population.*

The equation $x = x^n$, then, heralds proliferation; it announces a land of milk and honey where everything is available at all times in unlimited supply. That said, the promise of total accessibility harbors a threat, too. The digital universe stands before a gaping void, a fantasy of global destruction that releases all manner of demons. Although analog reality will survive digitization, we can already sense that it is deteriorating into an atrophied likeness—a facade or ashen shadow—of itself. In its digital mode of presentation, reality's effects are far more potent: seemingly infinite, lasting forever, everywhere.

Nor does the Boolean formula bear on the virtual sphere alone. Retroactively, it affects the phantasms that structure our reality. It encompasses the "real economy"; it transforms our bodies and our understanding of identity and freedom; it pervades politics; and it changes how we perceive time and space. It affects our very humanity. In this sense, the world around us has long since followed the Boolean mantra: *Through the Zero and the One all things were made; without them nothing was made that has been made.*

The Darkroom of History

It is well known that the best way to hide a secret is to place it in plain view. Accordingly, our contemporary society of information, which measures everything in bits and bytes, remains blind to the meaning and origin of its own concept of information. The situation resembles that of money: it is simply taken as something given. Everyone depends on it, but no one asks how the mental continent on which our information society has settled came to enter the world in the first place. When Claude Shannon, the "father of information theory," published *The Mathematical Theory of Communication* in 1948, he applied what Boole, the British autodidact and mathematician, had published a century earlier. Shannon's contribution—and this point is remarkable—involved only engineering and application. His act of technological fertilization didn't even touch on what had prompted Boole to construct his intellectual edifice; therefore, his thoughts on it remained without consequence. This silence at the moment of triumph is all the more astonishing given that Boole's theory had prompted great commotion elsewhere. In 1879, when Gottlob Frege published his *Begriffsschrift*—a foundational work for analytic philosophy to this day—one of the first reviewers, the mathematician Ernst Schröder, described it as a mere "rewriting" of Boole's ideas. Embarrassed that he had not built the intellectual structure but simply adapted it for his own use, the author did everything in his power to downplay Boole's role in the Fregean Revolution.

In turn, Claude Shannon, when asked repeatedly about his eureka moment, dodged the question and claimed that if such a moment had occurred, he wouldn't even have known how to spell "eureka." And so, because we collectively imagine the computer, as a material entity, to be a product of the twentieth century—and not the nineteenth—Boole has now been forgotten by the computing world, even though every single programmer encounters his legacy daily in the form of Boolean operators.

When engineers—even those at the top of their game—don't know about the prehistory of their field, they may be given a pass. It is astonishing, however, that theorists often prove just as unaware of Boole's earthshaking contribution; that is, they don't ask the simple question of the origins of binary logic. This omission is all the stranger in that the British mathematician's impulse to make 0 and 1 the signifiers for binary logic involved removing the *representative* from mathematics—an operation as radical as chopping off the head of the king of France. Boole envisioned a kind of mathematics that would allow for calculations with apples and oranges—that is, allow for one to jump from one number system to another. Such a leap was made possible when he took the 0 and the 1 (the "royal couple of mathematics") out of any order of denotative logic—indeed, out of mathematics itself. In doing so, he made the 1 no longer stand for a quantity, but for a presence, and the 0 stand for an absence (of something—whatever it may be). The real revolution lies here: Boole's binary logic detaches itself from mathematics; it abandons the material quality of what it describes. Because it oscillates between the universe and the void, it can describe anything. Viewed in this light, Boolean thinking is not algebra so much as a general theory of signs—a point the American philosopher and mathematician Charles Sanders Peirce grasped when he set Boole's *Laws of Thought* alongside the Kantian *a priori*. In fact, this same abstractness is what fascinated readers of Shannon's *Mathematical Theory of Communication* a good hundred years later, and today it is what allows us to digitize not only texts, images, and sounds, but also earthquakes, brain activity, and extraterrestrial phenomena.

Here, a convulsion that shook eighteenth-century thought comes into play, the lightning bolt that enabled the "New Prometheus," Doctor Frankenstein, to bring his monster to life: electricity. Not only did harnessing electricity prompt scientists like Galvani to reflect on "vital force"; by way of new communications technologies, it exploded the concept of writing. Anything that can be electrified can yield a script. In this regard, the image associated with the formula $x = x^n$ goes back to 1746: in northern France, six hundred monks gathered in an immense circle on a field, connected themselves with a wire, and went into collective seizures when one of them touched a battery—or, more precisely, the newly discovered Leyden jar. The experiment offers the primal scene for what led Claude Shannon, Boolean logic in hand, to his theory of relay and switching circuits; the only difference is that the circuit the monks formed was not a matter of mathematical calculation.

God Is a DJ

If, as Feuerbach taught, human beings devise their own gods, the craft they assign them gives each deity an exemplary characteristic. Here, at the intersection between rationality and theology, we encounter the same techno-enthusiasm that works its magic every day of the week in our own world. It follows that humankind invented God to deify the technology of the times—to grant the current state of knowledge a metaphysical patent of nobility. If the Greeks, with their alphabet, paved the way for the theology of *logos*, medieval Europe retooled the Christian God as a clockmaker. Since the computer represents a universal machine—like the alphabet and clockwork—it's no wonder that the computer pioneer Charles Babbage (1797–1871) tried his hand, before anything else, at a proof of the existence of God meant to replace the idea of a mechanical demiurge. According to Babbage, God can count incrementally in a regular manner (1, 2, 3 … 1,000), but He can also switch to another counting method (1,000 1/3, 1,000 2/3, etc.); what elevates God the Programmer over God the Clockmaker lies in this *capacity for program change*. In other words: *God is a DJ.* Indeed, Babbage's Analytical Engine—which employed punch-card technology already used in Jacquard looms—could perform just such a program change. But for all that, the Analytical Engine's operative logic still depended on an antiquated conception of numbers (the decimal system, which occasioned enormous mechanical difficulties and ultimately meant that the computer was not invented during the nineteenth century). Had Babbage been familiar with the ideas of his contemporary Boole, a punch-card computer could conceivably have been built in his lifetime.

All the same, Babbage's proof of the existence of God anticipated the defining feature of Boolean logic. If we compare the Divine DJ to His medieval forerunner, the Clockmaker, it is clear that the world no longer represents the mechanical continuation of one and the same law; instead, it is conceived as a form of change—as a genetic algorithm. Because x^n implies the idea of infinitesimal optimization, the logic has consequences for evolutionary thinking and the philosophy of history. In the nineteenth century, it found expression as Hegelian world spirit and Darwinian theory. Today, its certainty about the future is expressed by the credo announcing every new startup: *Make the world a better place!*

Everything Turns into Writing

What is x? It's obvious: a written sign. Following our conventional way of thinking, writing is supposed to describe reality. If it manages to do so, a given body of writing counts as the fitting representation of a state of affairs, a society— or the world. But this kind of accounting, where the world and the image face each other like the painter and his model, is rendered obsolete by the formula. The programmer no longer portrays the world; instead, he intervenes in the world. The x is no longer a written sign detached from what it signifies, but an electronic formation that uncannily twins what it denotes.

Already by the middle of the eighteenth century, the primacy of alphabetic writing proved questionable: anything and everything that admitted electrification could yield a written sign. It is no coincidence that, after poets began examining their neuroses and Franz Anton Mesmer had magnetized nervous members of the nobility, Mary Shelley's fantasy saw scientific practice—which could make a rabbit die, then bring it back to life with a jolt of electricity— as a monster stitched together out of dead bodies roused to a waking state by a charge. With telegraphy, the telephone, film, X-rays, and magnetic resonance microscopy, writing dug deeper and deeper into the tissue of the world—all in keeping with quantum physicist Richard Feynman's dictum, "There's plenty of room at the bottom."

Description and inscription became one and the same: programming. Now, whether it's a matter of climate data, traffic flow, whale migration, or the composition of the stratosphere, our world has turned into a gigantic word-processor, orbited by satellites and shrouded by an ether of information. It's not just that *read* and *write* have combined into one as *écriture automatique*. This script extends beyond our sensory apparatus; by way of infrared or ultrasound, it penetrates frequency ranges we would not perceive at all with our bare senses. As such, the Boolean *removal of the representative* heralded the end of representation as an epistemological practice. Programming means no longer being content to describe the world—instead, one sets out to change it. But to do so, one needs to appreciate the extent to which the world itself has become an inscription: a vast corpus continually emitting data.

It sounds counterintuitive to say that when we run around in traffic looking at our smartphones, we appear as writing in the flesh—that we are a kind of *ambulatory cursor*. The old mind–body debate teaches that writing is that which is not corporeal: a pure sign, the bearer of Spirit. But if *aleph*—which was originally an ideogram designating a yoked ox—had to shed its corporeality in order to become an alphabetic sign, then x describes the opposite path. As if to make up for ages of privation, the sign is now in the process of incorporating everything, without distinction. Whatever can be digitized is getting digitized: alphanumeric signs, images, sounds, objects, and organs. And inasmuch as this means that x is pervading realms that escape our senses, the sign now seems to coincide with the thing itself. The old dichotomy between the world and the book dissolves in the program: a hybrid world emerges, in keeping with the vision of the cyborg, like an organ made by a 3D printer.

Infinite Exponentiation

What kind of weird equation is $x = x^n$, anyway? A mathematician might object that it represents a conditional equation, which can be applied only to certain numbers (in this case, 0 and 1). That said, one could also ask whether

$$x^2 = x^3 = x^4 = x^5$$

or, in applied format,

$$1 \times 1 = 1 \times 1 \times 1 = 1 \times 1 \times 1 \times 1 = 1 \times 1 \times 1 \times 1 \times 1,$$

really amounts to an equation. At any rate, our eyes take offense: clearly, the terms are unequal.

But the equation does not hold only for 0 and 1. It can also be applied to any digital condensate (*Digitalisat*). If we posit that x stands for a given file, the formula means that this *whatever it is* can be copied arbitrarily—at our discretion or utterly at random. At the same time, the infinite exponentiation involved turns the equals sign into a command: an assignment, or allotment. Indeed, all programming languages share this feature. If we write $a = 5$, then the value 5 is assigned to the variable a. The equation turns into a transformation. As such, our formula could be visualized more accurately as:

$$x \rightarrow x^2 \rightarrow x^n$$

What does this reworking mean? Perhaps it means that we can no longer conceive of the digital world in terms of equilibrium, as the world occupying a state of rest. Instead, we should emphasize the aspect of metamorphosis (the program change). The question arises, then, whether we're really facing a mathematical equation at all. Viewed in historical perspective, *equation* (*Gleichung*, in German) means reaching a commercial agreement: the process of bargaining that concludes with a handshake, a done deal. In a further, wholly logical development, the term came to signify a judicial decision—a verdict, sentence, or award of damages that ends the conflict between litigants. In this sense, a price functions as an *arbiter*, a social referee or umpire that settles possible disagreements about trade before they come up. Accordingly, the key metaphor for the equation, "making-equal," is the scale, which balances out two different things, yielding a measurement, number, and weight.

Thus, if we take offense at the Boolean equation, it is because the two things being weighed clearly are not equivalent: they are *unequal*, and obviously so.

Posing a simple question is all it takes to illustrate the break that the formula inaugurated: does any object, in the physical world as we know it, act in a manner analogous to the Boolean formula? The only conceivable answer would be a living cell undergoing division. Yet as we know, even this process does not occur ad infinitum; what's more, it requires a working metabolism. Leaving aside the metaphysical questions Boole had in mind when he baptized 1 "the universe" and 0 "nothingness," the example of the cell makes it clear that we cannot view matters in static terms; the issue requires a dynamic perspective. But if this is so, what is the equals sign's *power* of transformation? The answer is simple: the power of electricity. Electricity enables any sign to travel the world at the speed of light; likewise, it permits a vast array of signs to be copied in an instant. Needless to say, the laws of physics still apply, but since the transformation happens so fast, we cannot follow the logic of distribution. The equation is no longer an equation, but a *morph*. Here, the law of metamorphosis prevails.

2   THE APOCALYPSE OF SIGNS

Hydra

Every piece of information is a publication. It doesn't really matter what public it addresses. The potential audience for the digital sphere, the Internet, is always the whole world. The number of copies of a publication corresponds precisely to the number of interested parties; it is measured in hits or clicks. Information that spreads without any possible restraint takes the form of a hydra.

Hydra was the daughter of Typhon, the father of all monsters, and Echidna, the mother of all monsters. She inhabited the Lernaean swamp, guarding a submarine gateway to the underworld. Her blood was poisonous; even the tracks she left were poisonous. The Greeks said that Hydra had more heads than any artist could paint. When one of them was cut off, two more grew to replace it.

In historical perspective, Hydra was the epitome of unreason, embodying the vengeful spirit of chthonic deities resentful of the Olympians' presumption. Since then, Hydra has taken on a new form ($x = x^n$); now, she is a monster of reason. This means that reason itself—calculated information—has become thousand-headed and thousand-eyed. Hydra's electronic tracks cannot be deleted. Once the poison has entered the world, it is impossible to get rid of it.

A case in point is the British beautician who tweeted, with disarming naïveté, her take on world history: "If barraco barner is our president, why is he getting involved with Russia, scary." Within a few hours, this improperly formatted opinion, compounded with foul insults, had multiplied astronomically and precipitated a shitstorm. The event was hardly gladsome for the young woman; many a pedantic commentator would gladly have torn her tongue out of her head. But all in all, it typified the wily serpent's craft: if the modern swamp works through electronic media, cutting off one's own head will enable a thousand more to grow in its place. Anyone who wants a lot of attention should stick his or her head out not so much to make a statement (*Behauptung*) as to chop it off (*Enthauptung*). Surely it's no accident that ISIL, ISIS, or whatever it's called, has adopted this very stratagem.

Nor does it matter whether the attention is positive or negative. In the end, all that matters is the number of clicks. Donning a digital cloak of invisibility, a headless swordsman can perform further decapitations with greater ease. The warrior may think himself a Hercules, but he's already a Hydra. The essence of *ressentiment* spills forth: all the invidious malcontents and commentators spitting bile, basking in the light of their frankness and freedom of speech while waging a doomed war against their own, skyrocketing chances of acephalia. The shitstorm is *ressentiment*: a serpent always sprouting new heads according to the formula $x = x^n$.

Social platforms exploit the economy of attention in similar ways. Here, too, self-assertion is a matter of self-decapitation. Anyone who thinks that wordlets like *whew!* or *ugh!* amount to a message is the real winner. It's like limbo: the lower you go, the greater the glory.

Loss-free messages proliferating by the millions—in a word, virality—are the lifeblood of successful Internet-based business models. That's no secret. The *ultima ratio* is to draw as much attention as possible to items for sale. Conversely, addressees—that is, users—have to divide their mental energy between as many offerings as possible. As a result, *trolls*, whom site administrators banish from their domain, end up putting on new masks to continue their troublemaking. The heartbeat of the Hydra—reason in its most monstrous form—follows the formula $x = x^n$.

Dracula's Legacy

When the computer pioneer Alan Turing was convicted—*in the name of the queen*—for the crime of homosexuality and, in keeping with practices of the day, chemically castrated, he decided to leave this life behind. Like the title figure of the 1938 Disney film, he bit into a poisoned apple. But for all its eccentricity, the cryptographer's Snow White fantasy was more than a bizarre way of committing suicide. As the metaphysics of the glass coffin, the phantasm of the living sign, it represented the idea that a prince's kiss might yet rouse Sleeping Beauty to life again.

If we content ourselves with technical language—*analog–digital conversion*—to describe this magical transformation, it is easy to forget that a fairy-tale world opens up behind the looking-glass. Here, different laws hold than in reality. Even though our physical bodies must go the way of all flesh, the digitized double (x^n) promises that, *should we not have died, after all, we may yet wake again*—anywhere, and at any time. Cryonics allows us to have our bodies frozen, in the hope that medical technology will eventually allow us to be reanimated. (Walt Disney belongs to this future race, too.) Similarly, paleovirology uses DNA to "resurrect" viruses that went extinct ages ago.

The digital simulacra ensuring human survival in multimedia form produce an uncanny effect. All of a sudden, the present is teeming with the dead—their voices, actions, and dreams. Like Snow White, they all lie in a glass coffin, just waiting to be kissed back to life. One click is all it takes. As they wander in and out of our dreams, these electronic shadows start leading lives of their own—they crawl out of their graves and block the prospect of anything new. Thus, it is no coincidence that popular culture, inasmuch as it is written and recorded, does not focus on the unfamiliar so much as it reanimates the past: stitched-together, sampled body parts are roused to life again. Elvis forever! The question of immortality will not be decided at the gates of the Kingdom of Heaven. The answer is given already, here on Earth. With this in mind, it is clear how the 9/11 attackers wrote their epitaph in the image of the burning Twin Towers: an endless loop playing over and over in our collective imagination, even now. Suicide bombing is every bit as paradoxical as the death Alan Turing chose. It proves that the other world begins in this one, here: the attacker does not perish so much as receive the kiss of life with every news cycle.

Splitting the Atom

"Nuclear fission" refers to radioactive decay: the nucleus of an atom breaks down into two or more parts. When the radioactive matter achieves critical mass, it sets off a chain reaction: the process of decay releases immense amounts of energy. The energy formerly bound in the atom opens up a glowing future. It is hard not to see the process of splitting the atom at work in the formula $x = x^n$. Per se, a digitized object is a divided object. In splitting, it is preserved as communication, a message. The process of breaking down yields radiation: matter turns into energy. In a sense, an object like this radiates beyond its own materiality: it transforms into a sign charged with energy. The digitized object represents a state of energy—and, with it, the disintegration of the material thing itself.

This connection to nuclear fission is not just a metaphor. In August 1945—shortly after the first atomic bomb was dropped—the administrator superintending the Manhattan Project, Vannevar Bush, published the essay "As We May Think." The piece condensed the immense efforts that building the bomb had cost into tidy, intellectual terms. It had taken the coordinated work of thousands of scientists from a wide array of fields to do the job: the project exceeded the capacity of any single person ($x = atomos$ = individual), and it could be mastered only by a shared and divided mind—a collective (x^n). Indeed, as a vision for a collective knowledge-system, "As We May Think" might stand as the founding manifesto for the Internet. "A record, if it is to be useful to science, must be continuously extended, it must be stored, and above all it must be consulted," Bush declared. Accordingly, he envisioned a terminal that would enable scientists to retrieve all relevant data and see it together, on a screen. It is easy to recognize the devices we use today in this vision. Only this kind of machinery—the essay declares—will allow all the intellectual energy that has been released to be bundled back together into a single thought.

Pandemic

When it's said that a butterfly beating its wings at one end of the world can cause a hurricane at the other, this is not just the credo of chaos theory. It also describes the reality of our highly networked world. When an epidemic breaks out somewhere, it builds up—over the pathways of nerves and traffic interchanges—into a pandemic. It's telling that HIV spread via the flightpaths of Patient Zero, the Canadian flight attendant who kept track of his conquests in a journal. If these records helped determine the agent of infection back then, computer simulations now make it possible not just to track avian flu, for instance, but also to calculate its spread by means of flight schedules and traffic volume— and in advance. Physical networks pale in comparison to information networking. The Internet has given rise to a social body that functions as a gigantic library, indeed, as a global nervous system; each and every neuron or node communicates with others. Accordingly, any gesture inscribed in the system can take on a viral quality. Computer viruses digitally mimic biological viruses in order to exploit gaps in security. Likewise, emotions steered by crafty marketing experts or disinformation agencies can expand into pandemic tides of agitation. Outrage! Shitstorm! Gangnam style!

Working Memory

Every digitized hand motion disappears into working memory; from there, it can be reproduced, modified, and optimized. Replacing human labor with the work of machines—a practice formerly restricted to industry—now includes activities that once belonged to the intellectual sphere alone. Anything that admits description as a procedure and a system of rules (that is, anything that yields x) can be replaced; this includes classifying, evaluating, and filing reports. Nor is the working memory of computers just a technological module; it also contains social labor that has been remunerated only once. In essence, then, a given computer user has a machine park at his or her disposal that is larger and more flexible than anything a nineteenth-century factory owner ever had. When an artist uses a Photoshop filter, it may appear to be a specific task, or job, but it would be more accurate to understand the activity as a kind of *collective writing.* What's more, this logic does not concern only the work carried out by individuals; it affects software, too. Software is no longer *single source,* but a composite made up of various *libraries* and modules. Within every x, x^n is pulsing away. Inasmuch as this intelligence is no longer located on desktop computers and in offices, but has become part of our lifeworld by way of robots and *Smart-Things*, there is no limit to the extent of its impact. A sensor transmitting data over WiFi to an Internet server connects whatever it is monitoring to the Machine. In this way, the Machine incorporates wider and wider swaths of reality into working memory.

When machines have finally taken over all repetitive tasks, the only thing that will still count as labor will be whatever has *not yet* been digitized or still lies beyond the horizon of technological possibility.

3   THE ENGINE ROOM OF THE DIGITAL

Snow White's Coffin

The screens of laptops, smartphones, tablets, and so on form the glass wall through which we peer into the digital world—as if into an aquarium. At any rate, that's the illusion. But just as the relation can be inverted at some large-scale aquariums—that is, the visitor, and not the marine life, comes to be surrounded—it might just be that once we have arrived in digital space, we all wind up peering at the world through the glass wall of our screens. Even though we continue to sit in front of the screen, we're on the other side. The world—whatever it actually is—is *out there*, the uncanny remainder of all that has not yet been transferred into the symbolic dimension of the digital.

If so, then we dwell among ghosts, having locked ourselves up with them in the Snow White coffin of symbolic systems. Here, death is alive and life is dead: the promise of life—the organic facticity of the body—has gone over to the symbolic facticity of the digital machine. In the machine, no singularity exists: no identity, and therefore no dying or death, either. Here, there is no embodiment, and, as a result, none of the body's finitude: no finitude of existence and no finitude of potential. If only that were really all.

So what is the body still there for? According to Turing, who dreamed of uploading himself into a machine, the spirit would have nothing to do if no body existed: "The body provides something for the spirit to look after and use." Now, the machine, and not the body, is where the spirit, the world within, resides. Accordingly, we treat the body like an object, or, more accurately, like a lump of clay. The body does not beget the body; the mind—the machine—does. The *ultima ratio* for generation of this kind would be to clone an optimized body in the hope of "mass-producing" others with the same properties.

The Party Rally

Communism, Lenin declared, is Soviet power plus electrification. We can think of the wired monks mentioned at the outset as the historical backdrop for this statement. With the discovery of electricity, a new mass formation emerged: a national aggregate—field strength—to be roused to action by means of general mobilization. Indeed, Napoleonic conscription radically applied the electric shock that had jolted eighteenth-century societies; it is still the phantasm of modern regimes of power today. The message of the Civil Code was radically egalitarian. A mass formation cannot allow for privileges; it does away with the whole superstition that a society may be modern while remaining stuck in feudal relations. *Egalité, fraternité*—plus the *liberté* of being able to dissolve into the body and movement of the masses. All the same, it took a whole century before the crowd could finally achieve politico-aesthetic definition. Coordinating the national body means subordinating the collective to a will: from here on, the potentate may consider his word to be the law. If we read from left to right, then, $x = x^n$ can be viewed as the aesthetics of the Nuremberg Rally, mass marches, and deployments—the phantasm of the *Blitzkrieg*. It is not by chance that digitization leads to thinking in terms of populations, sheer numbers. That said, it is naïve for totalitarian regimes to assume that the expansion of power is an arbitrary matter. Viewed as the expression of a mass formation, Hitler does not represent any old mistake; he provided the perfect echo chamber for collective psychopathology. In 1748, the monk in charge of the experiment was the one who touched the electrified antenna and induced convulsions in his brethren; he not only catalyzed mass movement, but was *integrated* into the ranks. In contrast, two hundred years later the mass formation celebrated its own demise in the madness of its cult of personality and the Führer: $x^n = x$.

Zero-Eight-Fifteen: Run-of-the-Mill

What happens when single human beings no longer matter and a random sampling boiled down to a representative figure stands for the individual—a cipher with an army of ghosts in the background? This perspective yields the modern social being that nineteenth-century thought called the *homme moyen*, literature *the man of the crowd*, and philosophy *das Man*. Kant, the philosopher, still had to pore over the death registers of Königsberg to calculate the day he was likely to die. In contrast, *Gothaer Lebensversicherung*, the first-ever life insurance company, owed its social model to the mechanical art of calculation developed by the computer pioneer Babbage. With that, eighteenth-century political arithmetic—which rulers enlisted to ensure their military might—became statistics; its full import became clear inasmuch as it averted, for the collective, the inevitable end that private citizens hoped to avoid. In other words, the certainty of death transformed into life insurance: an invisible bond tying policy holders to each other like the cables connecting the electrified monks. Such was the birth of statistics, sociology, and all the other disciplines that view human existence not in terms of its endless variation but in terms of social mass. In nineteenth-century thought, the *average person* became the norm. Henceforth, deviations counted as disturbances to be explained by the laws of *error diffusion* and *standard distribution.* In turn, with the salvos bursting from the 08/15—a light and portable machine gun—a shocked society came to understand that death no longer amounted to a personal event so much as a kind of applied statistics. The demise of the heroic individual coincided with the unleashing of the man of the masses. In war, it took the form of mass slaughter; in peace, it meant ever-changing masks and roles: father, mother, taxpayer, underling, laborer, price-conscious consumer, vacationer, swinger, and so on. "I" is a target group, a flat-rate aggregate: $x = x^n$.

Organized Irresponsibility

In keeping with linguistic tradition, we still understand acting and action as the work of human hands, at least metaphorically. Electricity, however, makes acting a matter of telematic manipulation; it empties out human agency and gives rise to collective irresponsibility. If only one of five buttons for activating an electric chair is actually wired, all the operators may deem themselves innocent. The formula $x = x^n$ means that the act of pushing a button—even if it still represents an action in literal terms—is detached from the agent and represents the taking of an abstract measure; those involved count as exchangeable organs for execution. To act without being the one who performed the action: this is a defining feature of modern morality. Consequently, it's always possible to "talk your way out" of things: if I don't do it, somebody else will. Or, the other way around: if I don't do it, someone else will beat me to it.

But the flipside of disintegrating agency and action is a law of empowerment: social power reaches a level of concentration beyond measure. The exploits of MafiaBoy, who used a denial-of-service program called Rivolta to disable corporate websites, show that a social strike can be performed in all innocence—not as a political act, but as a schoolboy prank. Indeed, no push of a button is required; a timer is all it takes. The sense of responsibility dissipates and, by the same token, the action's effects recede from their author both spatially and temporally. The Internet has given rise to a complicated—if not entangled—context for taking action. Here, any intervention, inasmuch as it can spread globally, amounts to a social process. Every action stages a world premiere. Or the world's end. The Internet runs the electric-monk program: it processes human beings.

Market Penetration

Following the logic of mass production, a supplier provides consumers with a corresponding amount of one and the same item. If we understand this consortium as a power aggregate, it is not difficult to see the glimmer of feudal structures still at work. A strictly vertical architecture prevails: the CEO holds the position formerly occupied by kings in national monarchies. By this logic, the head of the firm functions as the *representative of general demand.* He is expected to recognize the needs of consumer hordes and to know how to satisfy them. How, then, has digitization—which aims to *do away with the representative*—affected the great corporations and their little kings? If we take the example of telecommunications companies, almost all of which used to be state monopolies, the answer could not be simpler. The ascendancy of the Internet caused massive losses to powerful entities whose scope had been almost unlimited. Yet how did it come to pass that an anarchic and unregulated entity managed to achieve greater efficiency than a rigorously structured organization, which had the upper hand?

The question touches on two issues that frequently overlap: open source and the network effect. If Linux, a free and communal undertaking, managed to compete with a billion-dollar enterprise like Microsoft, it is plain that the capitalist operating system no longer needs a centralized headquarters; the combined efforts of programmers across the globe yield better and more reliable results. What is the advantage of a decentralized network like this? In essence, we already have the answer: a network, like the hydra, has a thousand heads instead of one. Furthermore, general mobilization means that the old frontiers have collapsed. Where corporate logic once authorized only an appointed representative to perform a given action, open networks permit anyone involved to contribute to the task at hand. The old border between producers and consumers no longer stands: company secrets have been aired. But what proves decisive for making decentralized networks into entities far mightier than classic power aggregates is how exponential factors come into play. Robert Metcalfe, the inventor of the Ethernet (which is supposed to permeate the very air we breathe), posited the law that a network's value increases by the power of two in proportion to its number of users. In mathematical notation: $val = n\,(n-1)/2$. If a network with five members can yield ten connections, a network with twenty-five enables three hundred—and a network with a thousand members makes 499,500 connections possible. Should membership climb to 500,000, a practically unimaginable number of connections results: 125 billion. If we correlate this circumstance with our equation, bearing in mind that the equals sign marks a process occurring at the speed of light, we see that Metcalfe's formula refers to the power of n: $x \rightarrow x^5 \rightarrow x^{25} \rightarrow x^{1,000}$. As the power increases, so does the number of connections—and not in linear fashion, but exponentially. A net distributed among n nodes is stronger many times over—more tightly wound and resilient—than any traditional form of power bound to a central perspective. The density of telecommunication enables forms of diffusion that exceed planning and, indeed, defy any and all intentions. In the engine room of the digital, even a minor piece of information can grow into a world event. This is the appeal of social networks—which are nothing other than networks spun out of other networks.

The Social Body

The body has long been conceived along the lines of a machine: as clockwork during the Enlightenment, a steam engine in the industrial era, an electrical apparatus in the time of electromagnetic communication, and, more recently, as an electronic, or digital, instrument. Today, in the computer age, the body both is a machine and begets a machine. It is no longer identical with the mind or spirit, but with itself. As soon as the body detaches from its material singularity, it mutates and transforms from an abode for the individual soul into a field of experimentation for the collective psyche. It loses its identity and admits customization at will. Inasmuch as it vanishes as the site of singular, fateful embodiment, it turns into something public that faces competition. This circumstance also contributes to the fact that bodies are becoming more and more product-like and uniform. So that some difference continues to hold, the personal body gets decorated, ornamented, modified, and customized: *make yourself a better place.* But really, the body has disappeared. As a photograph or post, it is tested and compared—embellished and enhanced—in terms of its outer form; as the object of medicine, it represents a mesh of symptoms, whose interactions can be checked, monitored, and serviced more quickly and easily when available in digital format. The singular body has also disappeared inasmuch as it now serves a social body that, ultimately, animates the machine. That—and not for the sake of an individual's life—is the reason to keep it healthy. That is also why all bodily functions, including those of desire, are now being shared—and to excess. In the endless monotony of pornography, blather about digestion and bowel movements, fitness routines, ritualized cooking shows, and dramatic cosmetic surgery, the body is shared as an object of display in the media, the public sphere. Ground down into pixels, it becomes part of the social body—the intellectual property of the machine.

Showroom Identity

Identity means narrative, the sum of all the data concerning me: what I know and believe about myself, and what others know and believe about me. It is the sum of relevant statements about me, including those that are merely attributed to me—ones I claim are hearsay.

Technological society has opposing motivations and goals. For the body to maintain its integrity, technology screens it off and protects it as a unit. The space capsule illustrates this aspect: a body launched into outer space is entirely screened off from its surroundings; it occupies a sac of synthetic amniotic fluid. In everyday life, too, we protect the body from exposure: food is getting softer, clothing is made to be more comfortable and multipurpose, and domestic space is growing cozier; houses are so many little biospheres, cars drive themselves, and hotels have all the amenities of the womb. One could even say that technology is trying to keep the body from entering the world in the first place. Digital technologies display the same tendency. Above all, they simulate the world in order to avoid taxing the body, while still leaving a safe space for experience. In the digital dimension, we shed our mortal frames and become angels. (There are already some who say that digital space is God.)

But in the digital world—in the data dimension— technology also demonstrates another tendency: to wit, fragmentation, atomization. Such scattering represents the precondition for elements to be assembled at will, or to specification, to produce synthetic material: *Kunststoff*, in German (literally, "art stuff," but in fact "plastic"). Such synthetic artistry serves to encapsulate the body again—to cut it off from the reality that beleaguers it.

The data world is always breaking down the body—the bearer of identity and active substance—into smaller and smaller units, which are then aggregated into patterns. As such, it and its behavior can easily be recombined into an array of new arrangements.

And so, in the machine—in the digital sphere—one can assemble a dream body. The body becomes a recombinable plaything and, with that, a design problem. Now, identity is no longer a matter of destiny, but a question of features, choices, and options. As the Newspeak slogan goes, it gets "customized," tailored to the customer's every wish. It is hardly by chance that in cosmetic medicine health and looks are so closely related. Here, the body is cut and sculpted following the conception of identity that the desiring machine has specified.

From this perspective, identity amounts to a composite that can be taken apart as so many samples—in the simplest case, by clicking *like*—and deposited in a databank as part of an anthropological pool. The algorithms of psychosocial fact that emerge can then be put together and fitted out in new aggregates, which are unlimited in number. The result is showroom identities à la Conchita Wurst.

Nor does the process stop there. In the digital realm that the Boolean formula has spread far and wide, identity no longer refers to something singular. Instead, it's pointillistic—something composed, ad hoc, of particularities found in the anthropological data pool. Like aliens in the movies, made out of shimmering points of light: $x = x^n$.

4 DIGITAL PLAGUES

The Logic of Decomposition
If codes—say, the alphabet—were created to break the world down into distinct units and rework them into legible reality, then this process amounts to a kind of digestion. The code decomposes the world into discrete building blocks, places them in sequence along an arrow of time, and makes them readable, interpretable, and, ultimately, programmable. Like a spider's prey injected with gastric juices, the world dissolves. From this point on, it can be shaped and molded. In other words, the alphabetic code breaks down the *world* by breaking it into distinct elements (peptides) and reworking them into *reality*, usable matter. Inasmuch as this demiurgic principle dissolves the riddle of Creation, the principles of use and exploitation—that is, extracting, potentiating, and transforming isolated elements—come to be posited absolutely and taken to be second nature. Enigmatic Creation is replaced by simple, docile matter. It is no accident that money came into being at the same time as the alphabet. Money is another peptide, which helps break down the world into discrete parts that then can be enriched, accumulated, and put back together in practically unlimited ways.

Today, the digital code is eating up the linear, alphabetic code. If the alphabet once served to change the body of the world (*soma*) into a sign (*sema*), the digital code is now going still further and dissolving the world of signs (*sema*) into digits (*bits*). Thomas Hobbes wrote, "In the philosophy of nature, I cannot begin better ... than from *privation*; that is, from feigning the world to be annihilated"; in this light, the liquidation of signs, their digitization, signifies a second-order annihilation of the world. This recoding proves all the more radical—this holds for DNA, too—in being able to erect a system of signs where a body formerly stood. It is not by chance that, wherever the world is transfigured into digital copy, ideas of a second genesis—optimized Creation—emerge. In the digitized realm, as in synthetic biology, the body is not broken down and recombined in its material form; instead (as in the case of designer babies), it is drafted as a kind of wish formation. But when the very construction of the body becomes a matter of design, the body (as a destiny) falls mute and can be experienced only to the extent that it constitutes a social body. Digitization disintegrates the body as a physical phenomenon and transfers it (big data) into a world of signs; there, it loses all definition. The body turns into pure information, a site of transition, where intentions, actions, and ideas manifest themselves only in passing. Even when one particular body proves lucky enough to have been preferred to a host of rejected possibilities, it remains—as per genetic law—just one particular body among all other bodies ($x^n \rightarrow x$); alternatively, it amounts to a particular body standing in for the population as a whole ($x \leftarrow x^n$).

The Great Flood

The simultaneous presence of all that has ever been created, medieval theology taught, *is Hell*. Under these auspices, the Internet may be understood as a site of world constipation: a digital inferno. The Net never forgets. And even when the party in charge of one server or another takes care to keep his digital lawn free of unseemly waste, the prevailing logic of proliferation ensures that each and every item of data is destined to last forever. If, in the innocent childhood of the Internet, the scientific community was still inclined to view the swell of stored information as proof that universal knowledge was growing, it is now clear that apathy, malice, and superstition are spreading as much—if not more—than before. In Hell, of course, all such depravity is part of universal knowledge, too. Toward the end of his life, Flaubert toyed with the idea of writing an encyclopedia of stupidity. If he rose from the grave today, Flaubert would have to admit that this work has long since been done—worse still, that it's constantly being rewritten and expanded. Information means advertising, philosophy, photos, threads, posts, and shops. It includes decapitation videos, funny cats, vanilla sex, hate-filled comments, high-end liquor sales, and front-page news. The whole landscape of Dante's Inferno opens wide—except that the Net has done away with the circles that once provided orientation for the medieval pilgrim. Moreover, systematic falsification and disinformation—which, in this deluge, are no longer identifiable as such—cause tsunami-like waves of agitation. Marketing firms and governmental agencies make virtuosic displays of how such quakes in social networks can serve the interests of propaganda.

The most powerful effect of information overkill, perhaps, is that users feel they can lay hold of this flotsam at any time and, consequently, no longer bother committing anything to memory. Indeed, they fall deaf to temporal depth—to historical consciousness. How did Alexander Kluge put it? "The attack of the present on the rest of time."

Total Liquidation

Since the start of the computer age—since 1970—money has no longer resided in (a) capital; rather, as a free-floating formation, it has become placeless. Once upon a time, the steel walls of Fort Knox, housing a great reserve of gold, fed the illusion that money is not an arbitrary sign but instead represents a concrete value. But now, the headless markets of world finance determine the value of any given currency. In the same way that our economy has become fluid, money has liquefied and become an electronic, digital sign. Indeed, money exemplifies the digital sign: it violates borders, oozes in, and penetrates every last pore of not just the economy but even the way we perceive the world. On the one hand, this development gives rise to hopes for exorbitant profits; on the other hand, the promise of added value yields the threat of inflation (x^n). Such instability—which finds expression in increasingly common stock-market and currency crises—is not an aberration to be blamed on the greed of particulars; instead, it is inherent in digital logic. Inasmuch as money, in keeping with the logic of $x = x^n$, operates at the speed of light, conflict necessarily arises between capital and labor: between the global, atopic sign and backward nation-states. As a result, the *handmaidens of capital* (as they used to be called) needn't even be particularly malicious. They need only carry out the rationality inherent in digital logic—when decisions aren't just left to algorithms for high-speed trading or risk minimization. Capital then flows to wherever the lowest tax burden holds and the greatest profits may be expected. The most recent financial crisis made plain the effects of this mechanism: money was (or is) no longer invested in the "real economy," but in the financial sector. As such, money spawns more money, while the "real economy"—the relic of an age in decline—is sucked dry. Today, revenue in the financial economy—that is, the economy that operates with placeless signs—is roughly seventy times greater than revenue in the "real economy."

The Attention Economy

If money, transformed into an electronic sign, is no longer underwritten by anything but itself, then viewing its function as a matter of measuring and storing value becomes problematic: the threat of inflation looms, and its harbingers arrive more and more often in the form of speculation bubbles. How can we preserve money's scarcity function? The answer is as follows: in the digital world, anything and everything is infinitely multipliable—except for the consumer's attention. It's impossible to read two books or watch two movies at the same time. In this context, the attention paid by the user/consumer takes the place of natural scarcity—say, the scarcity of gold. Such transubstantiation has given rise to the *attention economy.* When so-and-so many people click on a YouTube video, it receives a value. If, formerly, value was an act of purchase, now it is a "hit" or a click—some trace signaling that users have *devoted* attention to this particular object, site, or event. From here on out, value derives from the total amount of clicks (x^n) generated. In the attention economy, we encounter a strange dialectic: money is not covered by an equivalency in the framework of the formula, but is possible only given a natural limit. Only because the consumer's time is *limited* (in contrast to any and every digitized object) can the attention economy command any credibility. The analog (in other words, the human being, insofar as she or he is not x) underwrites the digital. The shift from a standard based on natural scarcity to one based on finite perception signals a far-reaching change. Value is no longer generated when something is wrested from nature; instead, it arises where, against the backdrop of superabundance, choosing one commodity or another counts as a significant act—as a display of belonging, lifestyle, narcissistic aggrandizement, or what-have-you. Once upon a time, commodities were material in nature. But today, opinions, perceptions, and emotions can be marketed—capitalism has taken root in psychic life. Capitalist rationality has not shifted so much as exploded. Wherever the economy involves rates, any and every object becomes a matter of shareholding. In this sense, all of today's talk about "Me, Inc." is hardly misguided: individuals stand exposed to permanent pressure from polls and quizzes—ratings rule. But at the same time, this means that we are facing a divided scheme of logic: on the one hand, we remain natural beings; on the other hand, we dissolve into digits that, in keeping with the logic of the formula, can be spread and multiplied at the speed of light.

That said, the image created by this process possesses value only inasmuch as it is covered by a *personality standard* with the same function as the gold standard of old. Indeed, Marx anticipated this problematic division when he observed that only human beings create added value. Wherever the machine comes into play, the profit rate tends toward zero; added value is possible only insofar as a human being introduces a *plus ultra*, which the machine cannot provide. But for all that, it is not really enough to declare that value comes about when and where the individual $\neq x$. Value results when a human being does something that a machine cannot do—it results from action eluding the logic of the formula (even though this same logic can help to convert it into a mass product). It is no accident, then, that the personality standard is not an abstract quantity, but instead shines forth in the face of celebrities: human beings offering performances that, while ultimately incomparable, are generally valued.

Illusory Production

It does little to help our understanding of contemporary capitalism to invoke the truism that capital is a voracious monster. The term *new economy* is much better suited to describing the change of the capitalist order: it signals that we've undergone a tectonic shift. But what, exactly, is this shift? For one, digitization has made it plain that the age of mass production is over. If unit labor costs for manufacturing further products tend toward zero, the formula $x = x^n$ sounds like a farewell to the classical economy. Anything that exists in surfeit is difficult to sell. The very success of capitalism has killed it. It is not just that products have become worthless patterns of uniformity, but that all the structural elements of classical capitalism, from human labor to the means of production, have undergone the same process of devaluation and hollowing out. The patient lying in intensive care is being kept alive by artificial means: scrapping incentives, aid packages, debt relief, and financial injections. If, in metropolitan temples of finance, the triumphant gestures of self-proclaimed Masters of the Universe once built towers rising to the heavens, economic crisis has revealed that these edifices are in fact giant tombstones, whose only real purpose is to cover up a historical nadir. The very phrase *real economy* points to the gaping abyss behind the Potemkin village. In a decisive sense, capitalism has drifted into the virtual sphere—where everything that happens involves simulated labor and *descriptions* of products and services. Even when it's still possible to exploit the rules of classical capitalism, profits tend toward zero. After all, perfect markets are entropic: the profit rate approaches nothing. That's why the magic word of the post-capitalist world is "disruption." Only causing disturbances in the market—be it by developing an entirely new service (e.g., cloud computing) or by digitizing an inherited business model (say, moving from taxis to Uber)—promises any gains.

Even though innovations and shocks of rationalization may elicit shouts of joy from portal operators, it's worth noting that even portals (= markets) used by hundreds of millions of people do not operate at a profit. If firms without a product manage to be successful all the same— by tying a significant number of users to their services— this means that *the user has become a product.* Accordingly, Facebook bought WhatsApp for 19 billion dollars—even though the company wasn't in the black and had no business model for monetization. In other words, Facebook handed over about forty-two dollars for each of WhatsApp's 450 million users at the time. In fact, portal operators are interested not in the market—where assorted vendors engage in competition—but in achieving a monopoly. The network effect can be exploited profitably only when the provider enjoys users' unrestricted attention. This involves a fundamental shift in the relationship between capital and labor: to harness the activities of followers (crowdsourcing), the provider must take the stage as a perfect administrator of the public interest, a kind of superuser. Even if he alone derives profit from the work that users provide, the social illusion must be preserved. As such, feudalistic thinking returns: following this logic, users serve as members of the provider's retinue. Providers no longer have anything to do with industrial barons. Their motto is "Don't be evil!" Their mental world is neo-feudalistic. Their religion? The gift.

Patented Life

If transformation is understood in terms of reproduction, one paradigm for the proliferation that the digital promises is agriculture. Inasmuch as it is concerned with increased yield above all, and since $x = x^n$ is a genetic formula, agriculture represents a kind of digital sphere *avant la lettre.* There used to be three cows in the barn, now it's a thousand. Five pigs were wallowing in the sty, now there are ten thousand. Seven or eight hens pecking away multiplied into one hundred thousand.

Genetic technology suggests that life is nothing more than a process of reading and writing. When the code in DNA is recombined or changed by human intervention, it counts as a kind of authorship. Thus, it is only logical that such "intellectual property" be patented. Indeed, federal judges in the United States have declared the work of copyists who transcribe and alter the original text to be a form of invention (which does not even presume full understanding of genetic structure). This lack of philological precision means that since the late 1970s, patents have been granted for genetically modified animals and plants. With this tool, companies like Monsanto have managed to bring whole markets under their control. Strictly speaking, modified genetic matter is patented not to protect a specific product, but to gain mastery over its distribution. As such, we can say that biotechnology is trying to apply the mad proliferation promised by the Boolean formula—$x = x^n$—to the "real economy." When genetic material is patented, the documents might concern an "invention," but in fact the real point is to patent the Boolean formula itself.

If trademarking forms of life represents the *ultima ratio* of modern society, it rests on a questionable equation of life and information. As such, it reflects the proof of the existence of God that comes with digital logic. If genetics has usurped the place of God, a brief look at the field's history reveals that the claim to have decoded the whole genome is a marketing trick: affirming authorial rights in spite of the fact that science has taken the very idea to absurd limits—and for some time now. After all, the exceedingly complex processes involved in translating the genetic code into phenotypical articulations and the interactions with other organisms that this entails hardly admit scientific description, much less juridical evaluation. What would happen if jurisprudence not only awarded rights to genetic *copy-pasters*, but also made them answer for the damage caused by their monsters? What court in this world would allow God to stand accused for the faults in Creation?

The Obsolete Human Being

Capitalism made the work ethic the basis of our self-understanding. Work is the ladder one climbs to reward and blessedness. That said, the history of capitalism also teaches that drop height grows in proportion to ascent. What's more, humankind has made a companion and competitor whose abilities already surpass the understanding and potential of most people: the machine. Whenever it is euphemistically declared that the human being has been liberated, the messy truth still holds that people, once set free, often plunge into moral nullity. Stripped of a station, the individual by turns resembles a useless creature of luxury or just tracks in dirt. If one tries to join the system again, it often means facing up to the fact that one has no prospects: working memory can recall the catalog of labors already performed, and it operates at a speed exceeding the human capacity for reaction. The formula $x = x^n$ heralds a world where we interact with constructs without any humanity: no fatigue, boredom, or moods. A computer isn't a *colleague*. It's actually a foreign body—and precisely insofar as it knows how to incorporate human labor and intelligence. If the Chinese company Foxconn, which assembles iPhones for Apple, has replaced its suicide-prone workforce with an army of robots, such measures follow from the logic of working memory, according to which the human being fundamentally amounts to a defective entity.

For ages, society made a point of equating human fulfillment with *industria.* Now, however, the bankruptcy of this virtuous image is plain. If we understand the logic of $x = x^n$ as capitalism's operating system, it is evident that added value arises only where the individual performs something surpassing the production level of machines. Since it's impossible for a single person to compete with the speed of working memory, all that remains for him or her are spheres where the machine has not (yet) achieved domination. Of course, there are still niches that elude digital logic; all the same, there's no doubt that these habitats (as sociotopes) are growing smaller and smaller. Even for somebody who—unlike most people—knows how to program the operating system of $x = x^n$, there is nowhere to hide. Once a task has been programmed, it lands in the museum of labor—and is devaluated accordingly. What Joseph Schumpeter called *creative destruction* boils down to a split. In the realm of the formula, we are faced with asymmetry: the human being, in keeping with human nature, can think the equation, but she or he cannot comply with it physically. Though the spirit is willing, the flesh is weak.

5 THE NEW JERUSALEM

A Document of the Universe

The founding document of the World Wide Web, its first site, calls it a "large universe of documents." *Universe* comes from Latin and means "turned-into-one." Here, all that comprises the world is supposed to be available. German, in turn, has the elegant term *Weltall*: "the all (whole) of the world." Placing the words side by side—*universe* and *Weltall*—we see two different aspects of the world corresponding to two aggregate states: on the one hand, the whole-as-one, and on the other, the whole-as-all-things, $x = x^n$. As such, the *universe of documents* (x^n) also stands as a *document of the universe* (x). It forms a parallel or mirror dimension where, in a great, global corpus, all documents about the world may be found.

The World Wide Web is not only the fulfillment of the Boolean formula, but also the realization of a collective fantasy reaching back farther than simple chronology would lead one to believe. The Internet has realized the dream that Vannevar Bush voiced in "As We May Think" (1945): a collective intelligence, where the labors of thousands of scientists appear on a single desktop—including the reflections and preliminary studies of pioneers such as Ted Nelson and Douglas Engelbart (from 1960 on). Here, at long last, Robert Metcalfe's Ethernet (1973) has taken shape—a vision that foresaw the worldwide networking of machines on a universal standard. All of this now stands as a positive fact in our lifeworld, and there is no escaping it. In a sense, then, the World Wide Web does not represent the beginning so much as the end of a lengthy process. It's the coffin of Snow White; instead of showing the world as it is—a nameless, dismembered mess—it presents Sleeping Beauty lying in state. When we set foot in this space, it seems we are stepping through the looking-glass. We enter a fairy-tale world that inspires the feeling of being not isolated individuals but part of a community. As such, the technological fancy that once wired monks into circuitry no longer belongs to the realm of experimentation: it is a fact confirmed by every click of the mouse. Activating a link, the user is teleported at the speed of light from one server to another—from Singapore to Palo Alto. Indeed, how the website appears often does not even correspond to a unified space; instead, it represents the simultaneity of different spatial points. And with that, the browser cashes a check that no physical body could ever pay: being at different locations on the globe at one and the same time.

This is where virtuality acquires added value. Having become the archive of the real, the Internet models reality and overrides it at the same time. It offers possible forms of reality. The process is rather like recognizing that you're dreaming—now, suddenly, you can direct what's happening. When you realize that you can fly, you leave one world behind and start to see other, parallel worlds, where other laws prevail: no gravity, say, or lack of resources ... Welcome, gamers!

The Sky Is Blue

When a tourist travels somewhere and takes a picture that is already in a guidebook, she or he is not just looking for an encounter with the world; instead, this person is collaborating, along with millions of other tourists, in a world simulation. The image will be posted, and at some point—out of legions of photos taken all over the globe—a pattern will emerge that might equal the world yet still have nothing to do with it. Nor are tourists the only ones participating in the project of world simulation. Anyone who takes pictures and uploads them is helping to launch the photographic capsule—and, with it, all that we normally consider to constitute the world—into digital space: a kind of ascension to heaven. Images that come in droves on the Net (Instagram alone charts some 40 million uploads every day) form an artificial "outer space"; atomized into isolated images, the world grows liquid and, in the process, creates an environment in which we feel as secure as an embryo in amniotic fluid. Just as the waters of the womb simulate a milieu corresponding to the ocean some 400 million years ago—the lifeworld, such as it was—the gazillions of photos posted today are making a sphere of images allowing us to think that we still are safe.

This liquidation of the world image can be understood as a social sculpture (though perhaps a watered-down version). Out of the images—this great vortex of digital "world substance"—it is not just the surface that precipitates and takes shape; rather, each one of the world's components becomes charged with energy that, for the sake of simplicity, we may call *psychosocial*. Like a liquid, it displays the colorations and covalencies of all that holds molecular fabric together and keeps things flexible. Whatever gets divided is shared and passed along for some purpose—however slight it may be. In the broadest sense, what circulates involves recognition: a strengthened social bond, self-confidence, a feeling of vitality, a sense of belonging to groups that have been chosen or count as predestined, and so on. The chosen images—their motifs, significance (i.e., upload potential), and communicative and aesthetic valencies—attest to the intentions, desires, expectations, fears, and anxieties of billions of people participating in the world-simulation project, whether they mean to do so or not. And all this energy finds its way into the great, amniotic whirl of the world that the Internet—a place for storage, work, and living life—represents. They are the stuff from which the new Jerusalem is being built.

That said, what washes ashore is artificial. Like the plastic detritus gathered in the Great Pacific Garbage Patch, rejected elements are producing a gigantic trash vortex of "world stuff."

The Best of All Worlds

When a random object is digitized, it becomes a population, a ghost army. This sheer magnitude (x^n)—provided that it does not strike one dead—opens the way for new modes of strategic thinking and ruse. One no longer stands facing the *obscure object of desire*, 1:1. Now the object forms part of a compliant host, subjugated to one's own desire. Inasmuch as infinitesimal calculations at the speed of light prevail in the realm of simulation, one can pit minimally different doubles against each other and pick out a solution that fulfills certain criteria (as in a game of chess, where moves promising the greatest success are chosen from among n possibilities). In turn, the model replaces the original—and the process begins all over again. Whereas Darwinian evolution—mutation and selection—is based on the natural cycle of generations, processors shrink this sequence down to a few milliseconds: with each processor cycle, a complete, evolutionary course of selection and exchange takes place. Even if the object presented to the user is a discrete unit (usually one with a version number), its individuality is just an illusion that has been distilled from a host of possibilities. It's like a voice rising up from a genetic chorus—a soloist belonging to an ensemble.

This way of thinking requires us to renounce time-honored terms such as *individual* or *atomos* (which both mean "indivisible"). More still, it means we have to revise our outlook in general: what is happening on an individual scale can be seamlessly transferred to the world. Not only does it entail the idea of *optimizing* nature; it also leads to working, almost as a matter of necessity, with the logic of parallel universes: entertaining various options that ultimately prove inferior to the optimum chosen. As such, virtuality does more than open a *second life*; it also discloses an interminable series of spaces: x^n possible worlds. Within the intellectual horizon disclosed by the formula, then, speaking of *the best of all possible worlds* does not express resigned insight into what cannot be changed. On the contrary: it signifies a formative will—what anthropologists try to explain with the idea of the Anthropocene. Yet at the same time—and this development remains historically unprecedented—the focus falls on the world. Looking through the lens of the formula is like looking at the world from the outside, through the camera-eyes of thousands of satellites. It means viewing the world not as something given, but as something to be made. Through genetic algorithms, the notion of generation known from ancient philosophy is roused to new life: the idea of spiritual conception, *logos spermatikos.*

Seventh Heaven

Just as messages sent over the Internet are allocated to data packages that then stream down to the target point as a BitTorrent, programs do not represent physical so much as *functional* unities. There's no need for them to rest on a hard disk as a memory block; in fact, they don't even need to be stored on the same server. A computer can download various modules from different servers and combine them into a program during runtime. (This process is now the standard with Internet sites.) If we step through the looking-glass, what stood before us as an *illusory unity* on the interface proves to be an object split through and through: a series of zeros and ones that have been divided into blocks, clusters, packets, domains, and ranges of validity. The inconsistency of such an arrangement does not pose a disadvantage; it represents the very condition for achieving the adaptability that is so prized today. The object is assembled "on the fly," as it were. As such, it is less an object than a cloud of particles, or a state of suspension.

This formation—in which it is easy to recognize our x^n—has a structure similar to the picture we have of the synaptic networks in our brains: a switchboard of various spatial points that come together as an *ephemeris*, an impermanent and transitory state. What is called *swarm intelligence*, then, does not represent a surface phenomenon, nor does it refer to an essentially social mode of being. It inheres in the program architecture of objects. In the nineteenth century, Babbage already identified the specific nature of this way of thinking: when we utter a word, it doesn't even take twenty-four hours for the particles we emit to circle the globe. Were it possible to design an apparatus for reading these *bits*, our atmosphere would yield a library of all that has ever been said. Indeed, one might even reproduce the words that Jesus spoke on the cross. If speech acts—and objects, too—are *up in the air*, the necessary consequence is for us to adopt a systemic, atmospheric point of view. It is not the particular object that matters, but how it is grouped with others—into a mesh, a tissue, a cloud.

Necromancy

In the German dictionary compiled by the Brothers Grimm, the entry for *Gespenst*—"ghost"—includes a less common meaning: "builders' scaffold." The authors quote an archaic source: "to make an arch requires much scaffolding, a whole ghost is erected." In this context, *Gespenst* is related to the word *spannen*, to "stretch" or "extend." Today, the scaffolding for building arches is called "falsework"—or, in German, *Leergerüst* (literally, "empty frame"). To build an arch, an appropriate frame is built and bricks are laid—or concrete poured. Once the building material has been detached, the framework is removed and can be used again, if need be. Thus, the falsework does, in fact, resemble a ghost: the idea of what will become manifest and assume solid form in due course. Something similar happens when objects are transformed in electromagnetic space, except that the process occurs in reverse. What previously was solid—say, a stone arch, a bottle, or a hand—is broken down into a kind of scaffolding: a "wireframe."

Transposition into a wireframe means disintegrating the object into a quantity of spatial points (x^n). This yields a model admitting modification at will. Volume can be expanded or scaled down to microscopic dimensions. It can be fitted to any surface or "morphed" into something else during runtime (for instance, into one of the spectral forms that populate science fiction and horror movies). The builders' *ghost* is a tool for stretching out an idea and fixing it as a stable structure. The wireframe shifts such architectonic labor to the digital dimension. Now, any given object is just the description of a body, inside and out. When the construct finally materializes, it stands as the supplement of the inaugural data-object—an utterly arbitrary *expression.*

This displacement turns our conventional way of viewing the world upside down. *Factum* is replaced by *datum*—being by appearance. And so, what once was known as the "treachery of the object" returns: an animistic perspective. The things that surround us are not apprehended as inanimate objects so much as spiritual entities. Formerly, the natural sciences taught that any given item could be boiled down to a *hard core*—that is, they affirmed a materialist view of the world. In contrast, today's software gives us a web of data inhabited by a ghost. Any driver exasperated by a malfunctioning electronic system will have a thing or two to say about it—and his irritation doesn't concern the vehicle itself so much as whoever it was who programmed this "crap": inner life gone wrong.

Synthetic Material

In the nineteenth century, there were plenty of indications that things were getting spooky. The specter haunting Europe—and starting to unnerve the whole world—materialized as a veritable mania for naming, numbering, and classifying. All that crept on the earth or flew in the sky was labeled. Modern cartography took care of the last blanks on the map. The world was inventoried, archived, and granted its first double. But the mounting mass of data had to be processed and digested. Karl Marx, who spent his days at the British Library in London (taking notes from Babbage's writings), remarked in a letter: "I am a machine, condemned to devour books and then throw them, in a changed form, on the dunghill of history." Just a few miles away, Charles Darwin—sifting through vast quantities of information in an effort to find the golden thread running through the "inextricable web of nature"—likened himself to a machine, too.

But what is the thread tying history together? As Marx observed, philosophers had sought only to describe the world. Now, the task was to change it. In this sense, theoretical analysis is a form of deconstruction that aims to recombine individual particles into better forms. Accordingly, the dunghill of history is not an outhouse, but a factory where the manure, once it has been recycled, will lead to a brave new world.

That's why the world had to be broken down into its tiniest parts: atoms, chemical elements, and rules of economic and psychological regularity. Analyzing vast masses of data made it possible to identify the basic patterns underlying movements and actions without number. Indeed, the scientific positivism of the nineteenth century can be understood as a kind of procedure pursuing its own abolition. After all, the goal of research was to construct a machine, free of distortion and error, for granulating the world into finer and finer units—and ultimately dissolving them altogether; results include today's statistics, graphs, scores, and motion charts. Thus, when a sound has been broken down into a Fourier series, it can be resynthesized at will: the process gives rise to a world that is artificial per se. That's why manufacturers now have to specify that their product is "natural honey," without enhancements or additives. If the world has become artificial, it's not a matter of inert or inanimate objects; more and more, it involves living things—including the spermatozoa, eggs, or DNA of extinct animals that paleogeneticists are trying to bring back to life.

The Living Archive

From clay tablets to paper, microfilm, and digital copy: the forms assumed by institutional memory have become more and more immaterial over time. In a broader sense, institutional memory includes magazines, libraries, museums, arsenals, archives, and registries. In the age of representation—which is now drawing to a close—institutional memory has been viewed as a building, a storage area. Its epitome is the museum. Museums present collections that stand as the sediments of cultural achievement. By this means, society can retroactively call back, into the present, what it has done and what it has been: it can canonize its accomplishments. But in the digital realm, the nature of the archive changes. Systems of preservation and presentation that are organized according to a symbolic order—for instance, ordered alphabetically or chronologically—lose spatial and temporal points of reference. Even though we still speak of "addresses," the term now marks an ascription that no longer has a spatial equivalent, or else makes it ad hoc and subject to change. A digital archive is not a location one visits, where one finds exhibits at the ready; instead, it consists of scattered "displays" for retrieving material as a simulacrum.

In the digital archive, any given object loses its uniqueness, turning into a document that is available anywhere (x^n). As such, it exists free of context and can pop up in highly variable arrangements. The work of art—indeed, the image in general—loses its exemplary status; it occupies a "place" that depends on typologies, color schemes, and tagging systems. It ceases to attest to deeds and becomes a gestural element, a hieroglyph—part of a character set open for use. Just as the *Mona Lisa* has become a cultural icon that shows up in endless reworkings, communication about things is replacing the things themselves. In keeping with Wittgenstein's dictum ("the meaning of a word is its use"), meaning no longer lies in the artifact; instead, its significance derives from a discursive imbroglio: talk that the object, which itself is mute, evokes. Inasmuch as such discourse (interpretation, commentary, critique, and so on) is stored and can be connected to the original, a nexus—a kind of social agitation or arousal—emerges. Even if the item in question points to an individual author, the intensity of the responses it generates reveals that, in fact, it functions as an amplifier for collective desire. In this sense, the Internet—indeed, every database—embodies a kind of *living archive*: here, the present is packed away into a museum, but it can always be sampled, reanimated, and put on display again.

6 GENESIS 2.0

The Abolition of Wolves

If we take the Boolean formula not as a historical matrix made by human hands but as a *law of nature*, it is not a scientific fantasy that is being redeemed—or cashing out— but a religious one. Dissolved into information, the world is becoming a pure sign. It stands opposed to analog hiss, contamination—*all that noise.* When something becomes a sign, it achieves immortality; along with its earthly body, it sloughs off all the darkness that works against pure reason. If the Greek word *sarx* refers to the perishable "flesh," *sarcophagus* conjures up the idea of being buried alive in one's mortal frame. For the sake of immortal luminousness, the Gnostics sought to mortify their bodies. Today—under the spell of the pure, manipulable sign—we can see similar fantasies emerge. The difference is that these fantasies do not aim to reach a world beyond so much as they seek to implant this same beyond—already attained through digital signs— in our world here and now.

If a blind clockmaker—or, in terms more suited to the times, a sloppy processing plant—has made the creatures of this world, then improving the faulty code seems to be a good idea. From this perspective, the evolutionary process that nature implemented as simple tryouts—a matter of constant trial and error—invites proofreading and correction. Now, whatever resists the digital ideal of purity must be deleted or eliminated. Advocates of transhumanism have left no room for doubt that genetic engineering is not only desirable but heralds the creation of an earthly paradise. All that enhances the resiliency or fitness of life is hailed; hereditary illnesses are to be rectified—erased as so many scribal errors. Indeed, some thinkers take the writing phantasm so far that they want not only to subject human nature to thoroughgoing redesign, but to abolish all natural suffering, period. This is only logical. If humankind's lupine nature has been overcome, why not abolish wolves, too—indeed, why not get rid of predators in general? From the vantage point of comprehensive, universal happiness, what is a predator but an error of nature, a monstrosity, deserving to be wiped out?

Social Spawn

As a rule, digitizing natural objects still means making digital reproductions. However, big data has introduced a form of modeling that works exclusively with relations: the fact that *in some arbitrary respect, as per specification*, a similarity can be found between objects. If, for instance, one looks up all the words in a dictionary that are thirteen or nineteen letters long, the law uniting them has nothing to do with the words' meaning. The words constitute a group on the basis of a formal system for ordering a "population," a social structure. By the same token, all items displaying the same timestamp might be brought together under a single heading. "Structure," Roland Barthes wrote, "is therefore actually a simulacrum of the object, but a directed, interested simulacrum, since the imitated object makes something appear which remained invisible, or if one prefers, unintelligible in the natural object." For Barthes, structural logic was in the eye of the beholder. Now, we face structures emerging from the space between objects in a databank. The formula $x = x^n$—especially when it works out as $x = x^2 = x^3 = x^4$, etc.—opens up a dimension for new structures, new constructs, to take shape.

All this might seem rather abstract, yet the business models followed by social networks have long since spelled it out as a command. Even though we still speak of "friends," everybody knows that this group functions as a voting herd: a multiplier indicating a particular user's significance in terms of traffic. The result is striking: laws of friendship, which used to be informal, become elastic as soon as they are given notation and inscribed. Consequently, communities of fans now can simply be bought. Inasmuch as the new laws of friendship emerge as manipulable quantities, they expose the blind spot central to a certain ideology and image of humanity. Suddenly (as NSA metadata analyses have made clear), relations become visible that would have better remained hidden: who with whom, where and when. Friendship is the name for everything that one can count on yet defies calculation. When this paradox becomes formalized, the Other of capitalism vanishes.

Branded Children

When an object is digitized, it is no longer what it is, but what is assigned to it. It dies a symbolic death—death at the digital stake—and transforms into an object in a database.

As such, it can be multiplied and correlated with other objects. It can be deformed and morphed, and the data it comprises may serve as a control mechanism or blueprint for generating an entirely new object. If a species barrier exists in nature, the digital sphere—which dissolves everything into bits—makes no distinction between images, sounds, and letters. What the human sensorium apprehends as a matter of synesthesia (say, "hearing colors") is the law of the machine: everything can copulate with everything else. Once it is transformed into a database object, the object becomes part of a herd, a swarm. As an element of big data, it turns into a static pulse generator and contributes to the formation of templates: emergent patterns, emergent objects. As part of an assemblage, the object must admit strict identification. Accordingly, it receives an ID, a brand marker, specifying its place in the herd.

Such aggregation logic, which develops in databases—and nowhere else—is now spilling over into reality. Livestock farmers are using RFID (radio frequency identification) chips to watch over herds, count them, sort and breed them, market them, and optimize profitability. The IDs of animals are fed into databases along with information such as age, health, time to slaughter, and shearing, milk, or meat yield. In this way, the herd—which already represents big data's master plan—turns into a data model that admits further calibration on the basis of trial runs, limit cases, and forecasts. The same mechanisms are at work in logistics. Companies use tagging methods to group packages together and share information about transportation routes and scheduling possibilities. All of this corresponds to how information is shared on the Internet. And the same logic prevails in construction: data models are cycled through until the object in question has assumed the optimal form; only then is a decision made about what material to use for actually building it. In contrast to the natural world, where things already possess properties, abstract objects "seek out" materials that will fulfill ideals as fully as possible.

The change of perspective is decisive. An analog prototype no longer provides the starting point; instead, the realm of data opens a window onto the real world. This shift holds consequences for our social order, too. As part of a database, individuals turn into quantities to be calculated—in keeping with standard operating procedure for insurance calculations, tax brackets, market research, and epidemiology. In contrast to practices today that still use "paper models," the future will enlist data related to human beings in order to "optimize" society: people will no longer participate in communal life as decision-making actors, but as pulse generators; their micro-actions will factor into equations on a mass scale and go into effect as a kind of endocrinological dosage after the fact. Indeed, this type of mechanism is already at work. Consider Nielsen ratings, sales figures, illness rates, and other demographic data that determine what gets aired, manufactured, researched, and planned—thereby influencing what counts as reality. Should the same principle find elaboration along totalitarian lines, it would mean, in terms of our formula, that the individual (x), as part of a herd, gets fed into the datasphere and processed as x^n, vanishing into the crowd; then, at t^0—some point in time—she or he becomes x again, when assigned a place in society that digital calculation has deemed appropriate. A subcutaneous RFID chip, as the placeholder for the individual's identity, would operate in payment processes, security systems, health plans, and social welfare programs. By the same token, data connected with this ID would be collected and used to recognize general patterns of movement, behavior, illnesses, trends, preferences, and psychological dispositions.

In the Data Envelope
Angels, medieval thinking held, move so rapidly that if one of them needed to travel from Rome to Barcelona in bad weather, two raindrops would barely touch its wings. The Internet—especially in conjunction with mobile radio technology—has given us just such an angelic body. Even when, heavy-limbed, we trudge across the street, we are moving in an ether of information. We may still deem ourselves integral beings, but in fact we have long possessed *two* bodies that are independent of each other—and not just in terms of speed, but by nature. I can do as I wish with my natural body, but my "data body" travels on far darker terrain. Suppose, for instance, that the police are looking for me. The signal my data body emits will let the authorities track me down—and, if need be, liquidate me (by means of a drone, for instance).

As such, part of my person has dissolved into a data body. Or, more precisely, it manifests itself as a data body. If someone else—an institution or a program—manages to get hold of this second body, not only can purchases be made in my name; insofar as my social network is accessed, such capture may lead to my *social death.*

Thus, the problem of data security occupies the abyss between the ether, where my data body resides, and the physical world of objects. This gulf, which also represents a contradiction, enables legal entities—institutions like the NSA or companies like Google—to gain power over my data body: a form of *symbolic arrest*, or *habeas corpus.* It is impossible to resolve the dilemma, even if every kind of abuse could be prevented. As soon as I take advantage of the conveniences that come to the company of angels (navigation, search engines, and communication at the speed of light), I hand my data body over and make it public domain. Anyone who so desires can now track down my *vita* and texts—whatever I feed into the ether—and use the information to his or her own ends. The *networking of my data body*—like the wiring of eighteenth-century monks—represents the precondition for any number of applications that now seem indispensable insofar as they unite human beings into an angelic host of sublime sociability (under one flag or another).

At the same time, this social network dissolves everything I consider to constitute my identity. No one can claim that a given piece of information belongs to a determinate physical body in the data dimension; it might be assigned an address, but the blank space that the body forms has no purchase here. Ultimately, affirming *data sovereignty* would entail the collapse of all the comforts the angelic host enjoys. For that matter: would anyone crossing a wet field claim to have "authored" the tracks she or he leaves behind?

Mana

When we think of software, we think of something intangible: the *disappearance of things*. Such a vision of emptying-out resembles the sensation people had when they listened to CDs for the first time. A digital nothing became audible instead of crackling vinyl: palpable absence, as if the materiality of the object had faded. In this regard, the *disappearance of things* amounts, first and foremost, to a change in the way they are perceived. If the digital object allows itself to be copied at will, the idea of its irreplaceability, to say nothing of its uniqueness, is over and done. The formula $x = x^n$, then, describes how material existence disappears into its own superfluity. Things are viewed as virtually inflationary. They lose their value. If, during its first two decades of existence, the Internet depicted itself as "Pirate Bay"—a harbor of giveaway culture—this fact reflected our formula's economic rationale: it is inevitable that mere things will degrade into a pile of junk with no value at all.

For all that, people are still willing to pay for certain goods. But commodities are actually commodities only when they exude an aura extending beyond purely material worth. The object of desire must be fashionable, perfectly designed, and capable of being upgraded. A kind of intelligence is expected of things—an intelligent aura, if you will.

In consequence, when goods are acquired, it means purchasing not just the things themselves but a spiritual presence inscribed within them (in smartphones, tablets, navigation devices, intelligent cars, and so on). In turn, this spirit enters a relationship with the bearer of the object: it becomes a proxy, amplifier, icon for the owner's self-expression and self-discovery. What now comes into view is no longer the aura of the thing, but, as Walter Benjamin put it, that of its owner: "that ornamental halo in which he is enclosed as in a case."

Everything Speaks

If everything admitting electrification gets translated into writing, the process yields a language that the machine can understand and speak. The matter does not involve spoken language so much as nature as a whole. Panlingualism was no Romantic fantasy, then. The vision opened the way for the digital age, the discovery of a universal code: "It is not only man that speaks—the universe speaks, too—everything speaks—infinite languages" (Novalis). Nor is it just a matter of computers being programmed to recognize speech, faces, or motion. The machine transcends the human sensory apparatus, period—whether viewed in terms of events in the pico or nano realm, infrared images, or the meteorological data provided by satellites. This explosion of the dimensions of knowledge concerns not only how the world is stored, but also how the world is read. Because processors operate at the speed of light, masses of data that otherwise prove indigestible can be examined for characteristic patterns—say, to identify genetic defects, cerebral irregularities, or molecular defense mechanisms. The significance of all this does not involve expanding the field of human knowledge so much as the emergence of a nonhuman speaker. In other words, universal, digital language has granted the power of speech to the *race of devices*. A new dimension and a new actor need to be added to the question, *Qui parle?* To be sure, the intellectual achievements of artificial intelligence lag behind the motor capacities of machines (e.g., drones, self-driving cars, or war robots), but the simple fact that digital logic is able to *transpose* one language to another level heralds a seismic shift. Not only will this achievement enable human beings from different linguistic regions to speak to one another; digital machines will be able to communicate with other entities (animals, plants, and so on). A metalanguage is emerging that will not just permit human language and human knowledge to be measured, but also enable communication on a subatomic or interstellar level.

7 EXPULSION INTO PARADISE

The World at a Distance

A stick is good for keeping things at a distance. It expands the radius in which one can touch something else—an object or body—without being touched oneself. It's a long-range weapon and instrument enabling objects located at a distance to be manipulated and brought near, as needed. The equals sign in mathematical equations is a doubly arranged stick. It keeps unformed, uncalculated, and incalculable elements of the world distant and, at the same time, connects them to the body. It enables an as-yet chaotic, undissolved welter of objects to be manipulated and made commensurate with the physical world. More still, it furnishes a measure for metricating the universe and setting its elements into a standing relationship. As such, it is an instrument of power.

This kind of relationship between objects is no longer guaranteed in the digital dimension. Even if it seems otherwise, we no longer encounter the things of the world. They are no longer on the other side, behind the screen. In a theater, we already sit between the projector and the projection surface. In digital space, it's impossible to keep things at bay. We're in the thick of it—given over to Brownian motion. The formula $x = x^n$ means that we have been absorbed into multiplying, proliferating reproduction—a swarm. In the digital realm, space is no longer perspectival or arranged along fixed lines; it's immersive. In fact, we now *inhabit* the digital world in the truest sense—perhaps as we dwelled in space before we became human, before the stick was discovered. We sway in the swarm. The distance between us and material things either proves infinitely vast and impossible to bridge with any message, or it proves infinitely slight—as if it had vanished.

Here, in data space, we are the things themselves. No distance, no object, no contradiction exists. And so, insofar as we are like the things themselves—that is, disintegrated and reintegrated at one and the same time—we can entertain any relationship with them whatsoever. They can become big or small; theoretically, they may be scaled arbitrarily. As such, the Boolean formula signifies distribution that removes the world. Near and far have been superimposed, and we must endure the ambiguity and ambivalence that this entails: intimate life in long-distance relationships.

The Outer World of the Inner World

When we sit in front of a screen, our body stays outside. Mentally, we are behind the screen—up on the data cloud, out in data space. Viewed from this perspective, the world of things appears bizarre, slow, and refractory—somehow odd. Mentally, we occupy a fluid, digital realm, but our body inhabits a world where the treachery of the object, a certain physical objectionability, prevails. This state of affairs has consequences. Our inner thoughts, which are already fluid, are shifting more and more to the digital sphere. Photos, posts, messages, blogs, and emails are now what convey our sense of being, not our bodies. As such, inwardness no longer occupies the core of our physical existence; it has been outsourced into the cloud. Indeed, the body itself is increasingly being transferred into the sphere of data by way of its various functions. Blood pressure information, blood sugar levels, urine concentration, fertility calculations, and cybersex are moving physical sensation—once considered the inalienable core of individuality—into the realm of data. What's left?

When interiority abandons the body as a site of residence and wanders off into data space, it becomes what it always already was: virtual. After all, the world within is where desires are administrated. Proper management is called virtue, *virtus*. It involves mastering and moderating appetites: not repression so much as tactical and strategic deployment, an economy of restraint and targeted release. But it takes some room to restrain desires and still keep them alive: it takes the inner world. Inasmuch as interiority shifts to data space, where it can be more readily administrated—and especially by third parties (which is why institutions have always sought to gain power over it)—the body is set free. Now, the body no longer stands as the fortress of interiority. It has become the projection surface for the soul. Since the inner world is drifting off into the realm of data, the body is turning into the site where relics of psychic space manifest themselves. Tattoos and piercings—tribal designs, spiderwebs, mythological animals, souvenirs, snakes, dragons, ornamental patterns, and so on—fill up the junk room of the psyche and spill outside, onto the body. In a certain sense, this represents an act of resistance: if the inner world is becoming commensurate with data, at least the body can avoid the same fate. That said, such practices amount to weak, apotropaic magic against the ghosts of interiority now inhabiting the data dimension. In fact, the ghosts of the machine are haunting the body and making it, aesthetically and functionally, into another machine. Cosmetic operations, body shaping, and fitness regimes serve to smooth out unsightly remainders of the past. The body is being pulled to pieces.

Such optimization measures represent administrative actions now that the body has been fired from the position of safeguarding interiority. Once it is no longer governed by inner forces—once it has been liberated from the soul—the body can be reformatted as a product: smooth surfaces, ideal proportions, compatible features, and customized design. Indeed, it turns into a surface where the digital machine writes its code. The body becomes writing, a digital medium; it no longer expresses individuality so much as the potentiality of x's alterity evacuated to the power of n. *Alter ego*: the real me.

Adam and Eve

To the extent that the individual collapses when personal boundaries dissolve and stretch out into the realm of infinite possibility (x^n), it becomes necessary to compensate for the lack that results. A fitting match is required: the Other as a prosthesis for one's own self—a means of achieving narcissistic self-control. Here, online dating services enter the equation. They both contribute to, and operate by means of, interiority drifting off into the realm of data. By comparing profiles, dating sites claim to determine romantic and spiritual kinship between people (in other words, the compatibility of their inner worlds). But in fact, the actual purpose involves transferring the logic of shopping and commodity aesthetics to human relations. As a customer, the user may benefit from greater selection, but as an *object of desire* she or he also has to apply the laws of the market to him- or herself.

Insofar as one measures oneself according to a social *imago* (that is, the images of femininity and masculinity conveyed by Hollywood and advertising), one is obliged to "pimp" one's own *vita* as much as possible and adjust the image to a desirable role model. As such, tinkering with one's profile represents a form of self-fashioning like devising an artificial surrogate (an avatar). For anyone who signs up with a supposedly serious agency—say, one that caters to academics and financially robust elites—it proves impossible to avoid describing one's personality in terms of patterns, drawing up a catalog of qualities and features, and following schematic logic when assessing oneself and others. When the inner world is cataloged and inventoried like this, a kind of database psychology emerges. Now, inwardness amounts to a seal of approval or a price tag.

Thus, it is no accident that there are dating services like *Adopte un Mec* or *Shop a Man*, which make commodity aesthetics—the experience of shopping—the rule of the game. There are top-shelf models and dead weight; market value is determined on the basis of customers' voting behavior. Indeed, the object of desire is no longer obscure at all; instead, it dissolves into a statistical quantity (which can, in turn, function as a second-order attractor, fueling both desirability and self-promotion). Another response—which is just as unsurprising—involves applications like Tinder and BangWithFriends. Here, virtualization assumes even greater dimensions: a swipe on the touchscreen does away with the laborious matter of psychology altogether. Decisions occur quickly. If interest is "reciprocated," further contact can be made. Formerly, such encounters meant running the risk of rejection (and corresponding embarrassment). The trick of these applications is to make a match only after both parties have demonstrated interest. In a certain way, risk-free assignations give rise to behavior that would not occur in the real world.

Whatever law dating sites obey, they establish forms of communication corresponding to database logic ($x = x^n$). Because human beings are finite and have a determinate sex, they cannot fulfill a complete range of possibilities. In this sense, the individual is $x \neq x^n$. Under such conditions, it proves impossible to content oneself with just one other person. A series is required: x^n. In consequence, generalized suspicion comes to haunt any and every contact—one is all but obliged to view one's counterpart as a kind of *serial offender*. But doing so only amplifies one's own feelings of psychological inadequacy. The result is *second-order shame*, which follows not from bodily exposure so much as from a sense of failure to live up to a media image. Coming up short in the digital dimension amounts to a kind of nakedness. It's embarrassing that the unconscious of the machine has not achieved fuller realization—that one's actual body rejects its power to shape and mold.

Strokes

Durex, the condom company, has developed an application that allows partners to stimulate each other without touching; designed for foreplay, it uses special underwear to transform swiping and touching motions on a smartphone into strokes and tickles on the skin. A Japanese manufacturer has created his and hers masturbation robots: dildos and linings simulate sexually aroused organs in the most straightforward way; the robots can be operated by remote control (at least in terms of penetration speed) or perform preprogrammed functions. In the wake of the hype about virtual reality prompted by Oculus Rift, countless clips have surfaced that advertise the device by promising the illusion of coupling with the man or woman of one's dreams. There are now data gloves and data suits; it won't take long before they're put together and used for virtual sex. If the chaste assumption still prevails that all this will redound to the benefit of people in long-distance relationships, surely the real appeal is the prospect of being able to sleep with just about anyone (x^n). Nor is it difficult to foresee programs offering trysts of different shapes and kinds. There might be preprogrammed "tracks" combining various forms of sexual stimulation into *erotic hits.* Petting, pillow talk, different modes of kissing and penetration, squabbles, and reconciliation would turn up the heat like musical phrases, riffs, and bridges.

This is all quite banal. But insofar as such technology gathers and processes data in order to improve services and functions—insofar as the information flows into a mainstream and, in due dialectical course, into subcultural deviations—it will literally be possible to sleep with the whole world. Here, $x = x^n$ and $x^n = x$ means a universal orgasm. "Was it good for you?" might not be the real question. Maybe the postcoital issue will be different: *Save, Save as, Cancel.* And once the experience has been stored, push a button: *Play again.*

Borderliners

"The human being is a creature of distance," said Heidegger. As an unrefined natural product, the individual cannot realize all the possibilities she or he embodies. In consequence, this inherently defective entity has the task of making the best use of the possibilities that do arise. Becoming human is a *Bildungsroman.* But what, exactly, do these possibilities consist of? Once upon a time, the horizon of immediate experience set the limit for what we could know. But ever since the world has become estranged—made distant, placed at a remove—the realm of possibility has exploded. It is not simply that prostheses now enable us to reach beyond our sensory apparatus (for instance, when a scanning tunneling microscope lets us see how atoms interact).

Additionally, digitization allows for telepresence and global action incorporating the storehouse of empirical knowledge. *Whatever you want ...*

For that matter: if we are able to enhance memory and performance, why shouldn't we? Why, if the body's appearance is no longer a matter of fate, should we shrink from applying surgical measures of augmentation or insurance? As celebrities demonstrate in exemplary fashion, the possibilities are so vast that it's easy enough to succumb to an infinitesimal delirium ($x = x^n$). If we can be everywhere, why be anywhere at all? If sex partners or life partners are on sale, why have just one? And since we can be whatever we want, there's no need to be anything in particular. As a result, awareness of one's own limitations becomes all but synonymous with a sense of personal nullity. The *imago* flashing on the horizon of our dreams lies so far away that it assumes negative form: a psychological antipode sucking out what little is left of a devitalized husk.

Wherever the ego is a void (or, to use a tautology, a crossed-out x), the individual hopes for salvation by plunging into relationships that promise to reconstitute him or her as x. But borderline personality disorder (BPD) occurs when the digital system short-circuits. Perceiving him- or herself to be null and void, the sufferer seeks redemption through the One. Then, as soon as the One appears, it is experienced as an attack on the sufferer's realm of potential and rejected. From this perspective, BPD is the signature malady of our digital age: what happens when the formula fails. It represents the sole taboo still standing in the computerized world. Borderliners show us that bare presence ($x = 1$) offers nothing self-evident or reassuring; instead, it means experiencing the self as having been annihilated, a flat zero ($x = 0$). In response, they seek to make the systems of others crash ($0 = 1$).

Death by Selfie

The classical self-portrait was soul-searching. Artists set out to find the shadow behind the persona. In contrast, the selfie represents an act of self-forgetting: it perceives the shadow but tries to banish it behind the membrane formed by the image. That's why there are selfies at the Louvre with the *Mona Lisa* in the background, selfies with somebody threatening to jump off a bridge, and selfies at Auschwitz. The selfie proves that one has managed to survive the impositions of selfhood and singularity, after all. Hence all the smiling—even when there's not really anything to be happy about. The selfie doesn't say "I." It says "Me, too!" For this reason alone, it doesn't actually connect with classical self-portraits. It's not one's own gaze, but a foreign stare that governs the scene. Selfies are a call for attention; shooting them signals the wish to be taken in and made part of a community. I'm there—Germany, the World Cup, with the Pope! The selfie is skin protecting digital existence from the body. The case of a Polish couple in Portugal shows just how far it can go: taking a selfie on a cliff, they plummeted to their deaths. To be sure, this was an unusual event, a misfortune, but lives are risked all the time for the sake of a better upload. Warnings are disregarded in order to ascend to the digital heavens. In fact, a better picture might result from avoiding all scenery—not showing any backdrop at all. The sea seamlessly fusing with the skies—pure, undifferentiated space—is perfect for selfies. The picture turns into a pure sign, an *act* where the self can yield to oblivion. *Me, too!*—in the limpid, digital cosmos.

8 THE WORLD OF ANGELS

Digital Animism

My personal data is like my shadow: if you take it from me, you're stealing my soul. Could it be that the subconscious is laid out on a digital bier like a corpse? Does data "embody" the fallen self; is it to be safeguarded at any price? Why else does such uneasiness arise when information—clicks, searches, addresses, and traces of online movement—becomes public? Could it be that, under the cover of our many masks, we have entrusted more to the Net than we would tell even our nearest and dearest? But then, are our secrets even private? Isn't it true that media visibility has become obligatory—that irreverent self-portrayal represents a principle of social survival? So to whom does my shadow belong? Does all this amount to making a deal with the devil—with the dark, inscrutable side of power, Google or NSA? The former misuses my personal data for business—like a trafficker in souls. The latter pursues totalitarian aims, forging a digital panopticon to follow, surveil, and manipulate—to take away my freedom. In either case, I am being robbed. But what, exactly, is being stolen from me?

In the animistic worldview, the cosmos exists in two forms: a material world and a spiritual one. Now, our rationalist world has cast a spell over all the spirits; it releases spectral forms that, as products, no longer hold any relation to their point of origin. But from the vantage point of animism everything has two sides. Even if an object is merely an item of use, the donor's soul inheres in it. Accordingly, when someone gives me something and I fail to offer a fitting gift in return, the residue of the giver's soul starts to turn against me. A tension arises—a kind of voodoo economy. This model sheds new light on the generosity of the Internet. More still—and in much broader terms—it indicates that we are entering the epoch of digital animism. Accordingly, the friends teeming on my Facebook wall are not just carriers of information; they also bring along their *mana*—which is why they expect me to repay their friendly turns in kind.

In contrast to other versions of the return of the repressed, the digital dimension brings the spirit world back to life by technical means. Even if they seem to have been banished, ghosts now form a mass that can be archived, administrated, animated, manipulated, and mobilized. Whoever commands spectrally generated data rules human minds, too. Ultimately, this regime will bear on the natural world and administrate it via the laws of the large number, big data. If charitably inclined, one might rejoice that digital technology is animistic: here, the natural and spirit worlds are not divided. Such is the hope of the Californian *Weltanschauung*, which banks on transparency: the total, bilateral interpenetration of digital and physical space. From a critical perspective, however, digital technology— like all technology—represents a means for subjugating the real in order to escape it. As such, digital activities are not making the world a more spiritual place. They are trying to leave it behind—which is a matter of actual fact, as the physical universe grows more and more fluid. The command $x = x^n$ turns singular aspects of reality into a farce. To escape the tragedy this portends, the real retreats further and further into the ghostly, digital world. The electronic shadow—like the *hau* in Maori culture (the spirit within objects)—grows mightier than the thing itself. It turns into the actual unit of exchange, and objects—understood solely as articles of use (*taonga*)—offer little more than its pale gleam.

In a world imagined along the lines of traditional animism, it's the responsibility of human beings to make sure that the ghosts are happy. But when digital animism prevails, the ghosts start attending to human welfare ...

Psychopomp

Does digital space mark the outer limit, the precipice, where ships flying the flag of our worldview start falling into the abyss? Yes and no. Digital space is technological. As such, it makes the world something to be experienced as a symbolic system; at the same time, it also holds the world at a distance. Like every technological space, the digital realm is simultaneously reality and the underworld: it liquefies bodies and separates them from the spirit. As a psychopomp—a guider of souls—digital technology comforts mortals with the promise of life after, and by way of, the body's disappearance. Insofar as we hold the whole of our identity at the ready in a digital cloud—insofar as we post, store, and retrieve, whenever we wish, all that moves us and makes life worth living—we put ourselves in the hands of the psychopomp. The only thing we still believe in is the omnipresence of our identity inventory. In other words, we get immortality on credit in order to cheat the body—which is forgetful, prone to error, and perishable. We stand at the mercy of the psychopomp.

Yet this ambiguous deity is leading us to Hades—the realm of Orcus, god of punishment. Disembodied as we are, we now pay a price: nothing can be forgotten. All that constitutes our digital identity will haunt us forever. Copied and stored, it spreads over the vast digital domain in its entirety; even if it no longer seems to be there, it can still pop up, like a repressed memory. Omnipresence—the ubiquity of ghosts—is a symptom of $x = x^n$. It cashes in on the threat of Anonymous—payback. "We are Legion. We do not forgive. We do not forget. Expect us."

Everywhere at Once: A Fairy Tale
It would pose a challenge for an adventurer to pick two coordinates at random and then set out to reach this destination. It would not be a *genius locus*—a place beckoning with its beauty, the hospitality of the people there, its cuisine, monuments, or historical significance. It would be a wholly arbitrary spot on the map—maybe in the middle of the ocean, in the deepest jungle, or somewhere without any roads. It might lie in a gorge, in a city, or high up in the mountains.

But journeys of this kind are possible on Google Maps, which depicts the world in its entirety. With a simple click, just about any point on the globe can be sought out and viewed, at least as a satellite image. One can zoom in on the location—in some cases, fly over it in a 3D simulation, or even enter buildings. Floor plans are available—as are photographs taken by travelers, with information about sight lines. Eventually, by means of such pictures, the surface of the world will achieve photo-stereometric representation and be transcribed into a three-dimensional model. Sooner or later, as if we were playing a computer game, we'll be able to go anywhere at all with a click of the mouse: the middle of a desert, a crag in Karakorum, a Kyoto side street, or a wild game crossing in Patagonia. Even though our bodies will still occupy a determinate location, x, the whole of the earth's surface will virtually stand at our disposal, in x^n points.

Although it may sound a bit childish, this science-fiction scenario could be spun out even further. Visual simulations will provide a pleasant view, but we still won't be doing anything—that is, experiencing the place *in situ*. Yet by means of the power of thought—as technology already promises—we might telematically operate an anthropomorphic robot in, say, Caracas; it would talk, interact, and "party" with the people there—or other robots. It's not as crazy as it sounds, given that this is exactly what drone technology does for purposes of reconnaissance and warfare. Somewhere in the Nevada desert, CIA or military personnel are sitting in front of a screen and evaluating what the electric eyes of their drones permit them to see—which, if need be, is then destroyed. This marks the beginning of ubiquitous being-on-site that will change the relationship between our bodies and their actual location. It heralds a floating state: our bodies might occupy x, but potentially they'll be elsewhere, too: x^n.

Drone Fantasy

The drone is a nobody. The animal that lent its name to these machines is born from unfertilized eggs. In other words, it is parthenogenic. The drone is the technological manifestation of a floating state. When it's time to mate, the drones of different bee colonies fly to a single spot, but without settling there. They hover and wait for a chance. In aviation, the term *drone* originally stood for an unmanned object used for target practice: something to be shot out of the air as it flew by.

Because drones are unmanned and sometimes self-steering—and are not conceived anthropomorphically—they represent the veritable prototype of autarchic technology. Drones could be anywhere. Everywhere, there could be drones. They're like demons—hybrid beings that mediate between physical and virtual reality. The drone is the pixel as object. Its existence puts reality itself into a floating state.

Infinite Presence

Unix time started on January 1, 1970, at 00:00:00 (GMT), its zero point. Ever since, without interruption, it has been counted off at one-second intervals. When these very lines were written, the timestamp—the number of seconds recorded since January 1, 1970—stood at 1,409,905,919. This standard is used the world over to synchronize computers; it affords an independent time zone for the Internet. The timestamp provided by processors also counts in milliseconds. Thus, it is possible to pinpoint every action performed on an interface—be it the click of a mouse, the push of a button, or actions generated by programs (say, setting cookies or creating a file). "The Epoch," as Unix time is also known, is pure system time. It has nothing to do with the position of the sun, the revolutions of the earth, or the days, months, and years of the Gregorian calendar.

What's essential is that the timestamp steers the events in programs—and on interfaces. Program sequences, fade-ins, and fade-outs can be monitored, accelerated, expanded, or postponed in relation to this reference point. Programs function like machinery with interlocking cogs; they consist of series of commands and processing priorities. In other words, it's a matter of "reading off" distinct instructions that then are carried out in sequence. By breaking down processes into the smallest command units that can be linearly executed, it is possible to simulate spatial events (images) in timeframes lying in the millisecond range. This "atomic" structure of time enables the modification and recombination of every picture element (every program event) pixel by pixel. Time can be stretched, squeezed, distorted, and restacked at will. It can be reversed or looped. Accordingly, time need no longer be viewed as a succession of discrete, singular, and unrepeatable instants—as a string on the model of $a + b + c + d + e$. Instead, time multiplies: the linearity of its moments is transformed into a *nunc stans* that is constantly modifying itself. The process amounts, then, to a field. The formula describing the field is $x = x^n$. This field, where the simultaneity of all that has ever been created comes into view, may be described as infinite presence.

9 A WORLD WITH NO BEYOND

If this book employs religious metaphors, it is not because the authors wish to share any personal preferences, but because the digital world summons forth fantasies of a chiliastic, or apocalyptic, nature—which seem to stand opposed to digital rationality. Where does this strange charge come from? How is it that the machine, as if by magic, evokes figures of thought that are not rational and, indeed, sooner or later assume the status of articles of faith? It's not so important that the computer occupies a position in the tradition of cosmological proofs of the existence of God—or that Babbage reworked the clockmaker deity of old into a programmer. In historical perspective, digitization has opened a new *techno-logos*: a continent of thinking that, in a century and a half of existence, has made its power more than evident. If the expression weren't so hackneyed, one might speak of a *paradigm shift.* Let us simply observe that a revolution in our way of seeing the world has occurred. In intensity and scope, it equals the emergence of the mechanical worldview during the 1300s—which was not the event of a century so much as the event of a millennium. Needless to say: the term *event*, insofar as it suggests a pointillist perspective, is misleading, too; after all, continents emerge through a lengthy process. "We discover what we have invented," Vilém Flusser would say.

More and more, we are coming to realize that figures of thought rehearsed and repeated for centuries on end are falling victim to the digital revolution. In the grip of revolutionary zeal, techno-enthusiasts have declared a historical state of exception: the *singularity*. Meanwhile—in a kind of shock-induced paralysis—critics lament the soullessness of our brave new world. Both sides, however, appeal to religious modes of thinking—and thereby fail to grasp the *historical* nature of the process. Unlike oppositions such as blessing and curse or utopia and dystopia, what has been bestowed upon us is hardly a virus sent by an extraterrestrial intelligence. Instead, we face a historical phenomenon—a symbolic form that was made by human beings; thus, it too shall pass.

If the Boolean formula occupies a privileged position in the perspective that has emerged, this is because it makes clear—and as concisely as possible—which of the historical forms we have inherited must be replaced or rethought. The goal of *removing the representative from mathematics* has occurred on a much greater scale than Boole himself could ever have imagined. When the code of representation was rendered inoperative, a continent of thought charted for centuries started to break apart. What we view as writing, money, labor, knowledge, reproduction, nature, corporeality, power, and politics—the whole land mass of our thinking and our historical consciousness—founders on this formula.

In psychological terms, it is not difficult to understand those who wish *not* to stand exposed to this fissure in the fabric of time. After all, it means that we have to consign a significant portion of our inherited ideas and conventions to the "dunghill of history." Stubborn adherence to obsolete figures of thought might explain what would otherwise remain incomprehensible in our history-obsessed age: the fact that the basic formula of computer culture has remained practically unknown—and, conversely, every last relic of religion has come to fasten on the digital world.

Such *estrangement* has fatal consequences. Instead of acknowledging how digitization shapes and forms our circumstances, we complain and lament, but only the symptoms receive attention. We wonder about how digitization is affecting the labor market, book trade, livelihood of musicians, rates of youth violence, animal husbandry, or whatever else proves to be a problem. This brief list shows how we are not seeing the forest for the trees. Turning a blind eye affords a certain relief: the new—whether blessing or curse—is simply incorporated into our habitual patterns of thought in order to patch up a crumbling worldview. Yet such repression occurs at a price: it means releasing conceptual and terminological monsters into the world— freaks that only plunge our thinking deeper into darkness. In due course, the space inhabited by chimeras and ghosts turns into a seemingly primordial power, an impenetrable jungle.

With that, it seems, a tableau from an earlier time reappears—a vision associated with the emergence of another universal machine, which preceded the computer: automated gearwork. When the mechanical clock struck the hour in the Middle Ages, it was hailed as an apotheosis of reason. Nor was it by chance that the Christian God was retooled and worldly potentates advised to follow the example of His machine in matters of consistency, tact, and punctuality. And yet, when the *costs* of the triumphant capitalist-mechanistic worldview became clear, enthusiasm waned. The bell tolled, and the day belonged to preachers of repentance: men like Savonarola, who called for a return to the *status quo ante*. Needless to say, late-medieval society was hardly willing to give up the new achievements. Sooner or later, all the incendiary preaching went up in smoke. Still, society had to go about retrofitting Heaven in order to balance it with the dawning age and all its usury—matters incompatible with the Christian view of Creation, yet vital. Profiteers were granted a place in a newly tenanted mezzanine, Purgatory, where they could work off their sins and finally make it to Heaven, after all. Such a reconfiguration of the inherited worldview does not represent the exception—on the contrary. The fourteenth century witnessed a vast array of chimerical—indeed, schizophrenic—structures of thought, including the sale of indulgences, whose sole purpose was to reconcile incompatible mental universes.

In retrospect, such phenomena may strike us as bizarre—if not altogether incomprehensible. However, if the desire expressed by these chimeras is factored into the equation, we can see that they followed from amalgamating heterogeneous mental spheres in keeping with Jenny Holzer's apt dictum, "Protect me from what I want." Nor, for that matter, is such psychopathology limited to dark, medieval times. Today, it is celebrating a veritable resurrection. Take, for instance, *data sovereignty*—the idea, which emerged in the wake of the NSA scandal, that people have the right to self-determination with regard to their personal information. The concept of *data* derives from the digital world, a world of simulation. In contrast, the concept of *sovereignty* comes from the world of political representation. The sovereign is the one above whom *supera-neus*—nothing higher—stands. It's not hard to recognize the afterglow of regal majesty here. Inasmuch as the terms are joined, every Internet user has been anointed a *royal child of modernity.* But if we juxtapose this sublime image with the Boolean formula—which corrodes and undermines identitarian equations—the imbalance is striking: clearly, one may speak of sovereignty only by repudiating the laws of digital space.

Indeed, our stubborn insistence on data sovereignty amounts to an unacknowledged admission that sovereignty has vanished entirely—if it ever existed, at all. By the same token, *identity politics* points to the fact that identity has become an empty mass to be fashioned and negotiated at will. Both concepts—along with a host of other, fanciful notions—represent magic formulas supposed to cover up the historical rupture that we recognize but cannot accept. Users may enjoy the conveniences of the formula (copy-pasted genderswapping, simulated identities, and so on), but they cannot pay the price. Invoking concepts from the past is supposed to offer protection against the impositions of the present and preserve the illusion that, all in all, nothing has changed. Digital space thus turns into a *hinterworld* (which Nietzsche fittingly glossed as *metaphysics*): an outsourced sphere following different laws than those of our reality. As a psychic beyond, the digital universe offers a landing pad for free-floating metaphysical needs. And with that, the schizophrenic constitution of the late Middle Ages returns: willful blindness and repression on a collective scale.

That's why it's essential to know the basic formula of the digital: it offers an antidote when misguided metaphysics— metaphysics resulting from misinterpretation—lays hold of rationality and stifles it. As such, our insistence on the Boolean formula is simply meant to mark the *minima ratio* that human reason must observe.